OFF-THE-SHELF
Fabric Painting

30 SIMPLE RECIPES FOR GOURMET RESULTS

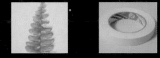

SUE BEEVERS

C&T PUBLISHING

Text © 2004 Sue Beevers
Artwork © 2004 C&T Publishing, Inc.

Publisher: Amy Marson
Editorial Director: Gailen Runge
Editor: Candie Frankel
Technical Editor: Karyn Hoyt-Culp
Copyeditor/Proofreader: Linda Dease Smith/Eva Simoni Erb
Cover Designer: Christina D. Jarumay
Design Director/Book Designer: Christina D. Jarumay
Illustrator: Jeffery Carrillo
Production Assistant: Kirstie L. McCormick
Photography: All flat quilt photographs by Sharon Risedorph.
All fabric and how-to photographs by C&T staff.
Published by C&T Publishing, Inc., P.O. Box 1456, Lafayette,
California 94549

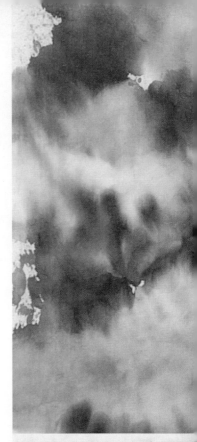

Front cover: *Fern Shadows* and *Fall* by Sue Beevers.
Back cover: *Old Chinese Bronze Leiwen*, *Swamp Arial View*, *Crosshatch*,
Sunshine and Shadows, and *Ocean* by Sue Beevers.

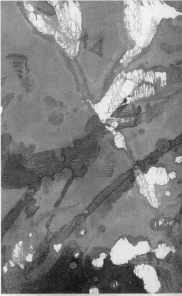

Library of Congress Cataloging-in-Publication Data
Beevers, Sue.
Off-the-shelf fabric painting : 30 simple recipes for gourmet results
/ Sue Beevers.
p. cm.
ISBN 1-57120-226-9 (paper trade)
1. Fabric painting. I. Title.
TT851.B44 2004
746.6–dc21
2003010288

Printed in China
10 9 8 7 6 5 4 3 2 1

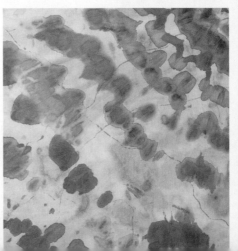

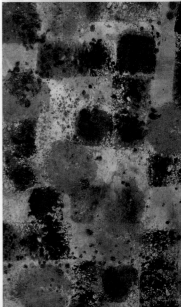

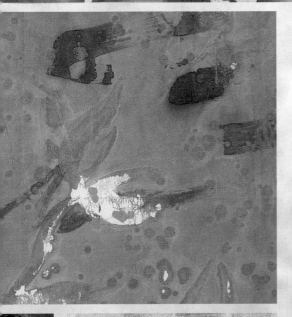

for David

ACKNOWLEDGMENTS

Writing a book is seldom a solitary venture. In my case, this book is a culmination of years and years of experience in the fiber field; a constant thirst for discovering "what if?"; countless hours of sharing ideas with spinning, dyeing, weaving, and quilting friends; and plenty of help from friends, relatives, and professionals.

I would especially like to thank the folks at C&T for giving me this opportunity and making it a pleasurable experience. In particular, I would like to thank editors Jan Grigsby and Candie Frankel for their support and constructive criticism, and Christina Jarumay for her marvelous book design.

I would like to thank everyone at PROchem, in particular Nancy Rodriguez, for reading the manuscript and checking for technical errors regarding their products.

Thank you also to Mike Townsend and Golden Artists Colors for technical information about their product lines.

Finally, I would like to thank the morning group—Kathryn, Gail, and Colleen—for their friendship, creativity, and encouragement.

Thank you.

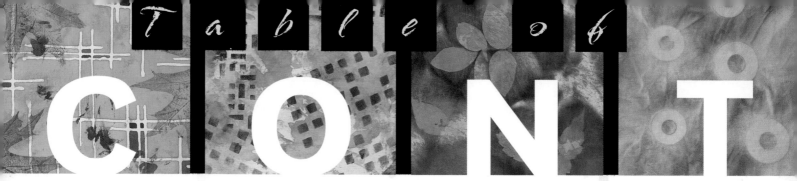

Table of CONT

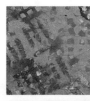

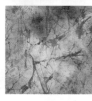
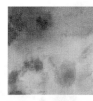

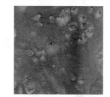

Introduction

I am an artist. I draw, paint, and make prints. I have also spent the last thirty years of my life immersed in the fiber field, first as a spinner, weaver, and dyer, and now as a fabric painter and quilter. I don't view these activities as individual, competing endeavors. Instead, I see them all as a means of self-expression.

I started painting fabrics before I started quilting. I work a lot with water media, and found that painting on fabric allowed me to express an idea in a way that was different from using paper or gessoed canvas. When I started quilting, I found that although there were marvelous commercial fabrics available, they often didn't meet my design needs. Painting allows me to create color combinations that are exactly what I want. It allows me to put visual texture exactly where I want it, exactly how I want it.

I see fabric design as a process: A fabric is often painted, dried, and then repainted, and I usually employ more than one technique. As a result, the creation of a single fabric evolves over a number of days. I usually work on more than one fabric at a time; while one is drying, I work on another. If a fabric isn't progressing as I wish it to, I set it aside for a few days and then come back to it. I can usually then see what needs to be done to make it complete.

Although my painted fabrics are intended for use in quilts, and will most likely be cut into pieces, I try to design each fabric as I would a painting. I feel that each fabric should be able to stand by itself as a visually interesting piece.

I seldom try to duplicate a fabric exactly. Most of my fabrics are used in quilts, and I find quilts that use a lot of different fabrics to be more exciting. Why use 20 fabrics when you can use 220?

Painting fabric is an exciting, creative endeavor, and I know that you want to dive right in. But I urge you to spend a few minutes with the first three chapters. It's important to understand how fabric paints behave, how to put color theory to practical use, and how to set up your painting studio—even if all you've got available is a kitchen counter-top. A little foreknowledge will ensure that your fabric painting experience is enjoyable and successful.

The painting techniques are organized into four sections. There are simple free-form techniques to get you started in your fabric paint explorations; marvelous background textures to use on their own or as a base for more involved applications; print techniques, including stamping and stenciling, for added visual texture; and resist techniques, accomplished with common household vegetal starches and by stitching, folding, and tying the fabrics.

I suggest trying the techniques in the order presented, as each one builds upon the ideas and skills presented previously. The step-by-step recipes and fabric samples in each chapter are your starting point, not your final destination. Use the recipes as a guide, and let your own creative energy shine through. For me, this is the most exciting part about fabric painting.

A final word, before you get started. Don't paint with a specific project or picture in mind. Instead, relive the fun that you had as a child making wandering lines, squiggles, and blotches. Free-form, abstract designs will allow you to concentrate all your creative energy into making beautiful fabric, without the worry of wondering if your painting looks "right." Play with the color, play with the paint, and experiment. This is how you will learn what works for you, and what doesn't.

Most of all, have fun.

PREPARING TO PAINT

FABRIC PAINTS

Any acrylic paint can be applied to fabric, but some products are better suited than others. For easy application and opaque coverage, the paint should have a high pigment load and a thick, workable consistency. Good-quality paint, properly set, will not rub off as the fabric is handled, used, and cleaned.

The painted fabrics you create for quiltmaking should be washable and colorfast. You want the fibers to retain the same softness and pliability they had before paint was applied. Unlike fabric dyes, which seep through and chemically bond with the fibers, paint sits on the surface. As a result, painted fabric often has a front and a back, with the front showing more pigment than the back. The challenge is to find a paint that does not stiffen the fibers as it colors them.

THREE FAVORITE BRANDS

After much experimentation, I have identified three brands of paint that fit my fabric painting needs. Each has unique properties, and each works particularly well in certain applications. The chart on page 93 compares the brands point by point and will help you in your selections. Any of the three brands will work for most of the recipes in this book; when a particular paint is required—for example, for sunprinting—the recipe will say so. I don't recommend mixing different brands together, since each one is formulated differently. When I want to use different brands on the same cloth, I allow the paint to dry thoroughly between applications.

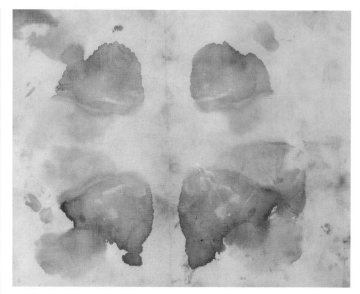

Golden Fluid Acrylic. The dilute transparent color does not separate easily.

■ **Golden Fluid Acrylic** is particularly suited to situations where dilute, transparent, watery colors are desired. This is because the pigment particles do not separate out as readily as they do in other brands. Intended mainly for use on paper and canvas, the paint is easily applied to fabric, especially when diluted with water or additives. Additives increase the open time of the paint and increase the washability of the painted fabric. The resulting fabrics have a soft hand. Conversely, the paint is less effective at producing rich, saturated color while maintaining a soft hand, especially when large areas are to be filled.

The palette of 51 colors runs the gamut from transparent to opaque. Quinacridone colors are most transparent, while pyrrole colors are very opaque. Phthalo colors have a very high pigment load but become quite transparent when diluted. Hansa colors are slightly opaque. My favorite color palette is anthroquinone blue, permanent violet dark, Jenkins green, quinacridone gold, phthalo turquoise, dioxizine purple, and quinacridone burnt orange. A brighter palette can be mixed with just 3 colors: Hansa yellow, pyrrole red, and phthalo blue (green shade). All the colors, especially those containing blue, will sunprint. There are also 10 interference and 10 iridescent colors.

■ **Pebeo Setacolor Textile Paint** is formulated specifically for fabrics. It comes in 21 transparent colors and 18 opaque colors. Opaque shimmer colors, fluorescent colors, and gold and silver glitter finishes are also available.

I find the transparent paint to be this brand's best product. I can mix a palette with a good color range using just seven colors: yellow, vermilion, orient red, violet, ultramarine, cobalt, and emerald. The paint is very easy to apply and control; it allows for saturated color while maintaining a soft hand. It also sunprints very easily. If this paint is highly diluted, however, the pigment particles will separate out and create a dusty appearance.

■ **PROfab Textile Paint** is my favorite opaque paint. It can be used straight from the jar, the coverage is truly opaque, not just semiopaque, and it dries quickly, so overlapping designs can be finished more quickly. The full line of 45 colors is available in transparent and opaque paints; there are also pearlescent and fluorescent colors. I can mix a palette with a nice range using 6 colors: opaque white, lemon yellow, golden yellow, red, blue, and leaf green.

This paint comes out of the container the consistency of mayonnaise—perfect for stenciling or stamping. For other applications, the paint can be thinned with LoCrock solution, which is a 3:1 mixture of water and LoCrock Concentrate. To lighten the color without altering the consistency, add PROfab Base Extender. Doing this will lessen the paint's opacity or increase its transparency, depending on how you want to think about it.

Another option from this manufacturer is **PROfab Color Concentrates**. These concentrated pigments must be mixed with either LoCrock solution or PROfab Base Extender in order to bond to the fabric. Using a concentrate gives me greater control over the consistency and color of the paints that I mix. It allows me, for example, to mix a very thin paint in a fully saturated color, something I cannot do with other paint brands. The manufacturer suggests mixing PROfab Color Concentrate with either 1 cup LoCrock solution, for a thin consistency, or 1 cup PROfab Base Extender, for a thick consistency. Use 2 teaspoons concentrate for a light color, 5 teaspoons for a medium color, and 8 teaspoons for a dark, fully saturated color.

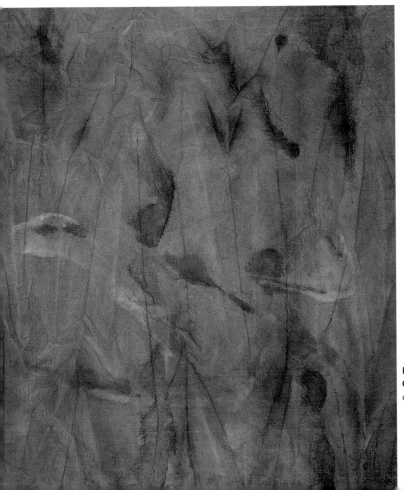

TRANSPARENT VS. OPAQUE

Transparent and opaque paints behave differently. Your painting experiments will be more productive if you understand in advance how each paint works and interacts.

Transparent paint acts a little like dye. It allows the cloth to show through, a feature that I find desirable. Water added to transparent paint will lighten it further. White paint added to transparent paint will lighten it and also increase the opacity somewhat. Generally, lighter transparent colors are applied to the fabric first, followed by darker ones. Previously painted colors will visually combine with newly painted ones. Care must be taken when choosing colors. Complementary colors, for example, will become muddy where they overlay one another.

Opaque paint, in contrast, does not allow the fabric or previously painted colors to show through. Because there is no show-through, color mixing is not an issue. Dark colors can be applied first, followed by lighter ones. Opaque colors are particularly good for stenciling and small details. Adding water to an opaque paint will lighten the color and lessen the opacity. Adding white paint to an opaque paint will lighten the color without affecting the opacity.

You should be aware that different paint colors, even within the same product line, will vary in their degree of transparency and opacity. You will need to experiment to discover how each color performs. Also keep in mind that water allows paint to spread on a fabric. Thin paint diffuses more readily than thick paint. Once paint is dry, its water content, or viscosity, will no longer be a factor. Only the color remains behind. It's important to keep this aspect of paint behavior in mind when layering paints and combining painting techniques.

Pebeo Transparent and PROfab Opaque Paint. The colors were allowed to dry between applications.

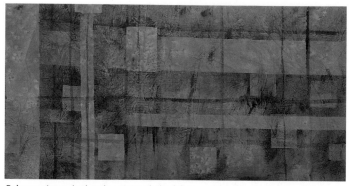

Pebeo paint, salted and sunprinted; the fabric was then masked and painted on a wrinkled surface with thickened Golden Fluid Acrylic.

Thin PROfab paint mixed from concentrate in various color saturation levels. Fabric salted while drying.

David's Garden, Sue Beevers, 2002, 41" x 41". Machine-pieced, paper-pieced, machine-embroidered, machine-quilted, beaded.

PRESERVING THE COLOR

All fabric paints must be allowed to set and stabilize before they are washed. Properly set colors will not rub off (called crocking) or wash out. Heat makes the color setting process go faster. **Heat setting** can be accomplished with:

■ **A clothes dryer**. Use a dryer that vents to the outdoors. Be aware that the heat-setting time recommended by the manufacturer does not take into account the cooldown, low-wrinkle cycle built into the drying time dial on many dryers. If your dryer has such a cycle, you'll need to reset the dial for the additional minutes before the dryer reaches the cool-down cycle.

■ **An oven**. This is the quickest method of heat setting, but not all manufacturers recommend it. Be sure to provide ample ventilation, as a trace of formaldehyde is released at the start of the process.

■ **An iron**. Work in a well-ventilated area. As with an oven, some noxious chemicals will outgas when heat is first applied to a newly painted, unwashed fabric.

After the paint colors are set, either with heat or by a passive set, the fabric must be washed to remove any residual chemicals and extra paint. Washing is usually done by hand rather than by machine. Machine agitation rubs the fabric and loosens tiny unpainted fibers, bringing them to the surface. This results in a subtle lightening of the color, a situation that is particularly noticeable with dark values. Hand washing and line drying are recommended to extend the life of a painted fabric in general.

Confined Color Mixing

PRACTICAL COLOR THEORY

The successful manipulation of color to suit a particular design goal is a combination of knowledge, skill, and experience. Learning about color theory is a good place to start. But remember, it is just a theory. Practical application is often different, particularly when the medium is wet, fluid paint. If you know what to expect, you're less likely to be disappointed or caught off-guard by experiments gone awry.

A key point to remember is that paint thinned with water or applied to a very wet fabric surface migrates readily. As wet paint colors migrate, they lose intensity. When wet colors touch one another, they blend together to form a new color. If you don't want particular colors to blend together where they touch, you must dry that section of the painted fabric before applying the second color.

Color theory will help you understand how certain colors can be blended to make new colors. It will also help you choose the colors you want to start out with. The recipes in this book all use generic color names, rather than manufacturer names, so that you can adapt the palettes to any brand of paint you choose. Your success as a fabric painter depends on your understanding of these principles and of each paint's idiosyncrasies. Making your own discoveries about color is what makes fabric painting fun.

THE COLOR WHEEL

The first thing to understand about color is that it can be divided into two groups: chromatic and achromatic. A color that is **chromatic** has color (chroma) and contains one or more of the colors of the spectrum. Black, white, and gray are **achromatic**, or absent of color—at least in theory.

As you begin working with paints, you will discover that the blacks are not pure black at all but lean toward blue or red. While pure white is possible in both paint and fabric, you'll most likely be working with "natural" fabric, which is actually quite yellow. Gray is obtained by mixing black and white (opaque paint) or black and water (transparent paint). Like blacks, painted grays lean either toward red (the warm grays) or toward blue (the cool grays). The tendency toward warm or cool can be easily seen when transparent black is diluted with water. Finally, black paint added to yellow makes green.

Chromatics are often diagrammed on a **color wheel**. There are many versions of the color wheel in past and present use. Each strives to be a visual representation of the relationships between colors.

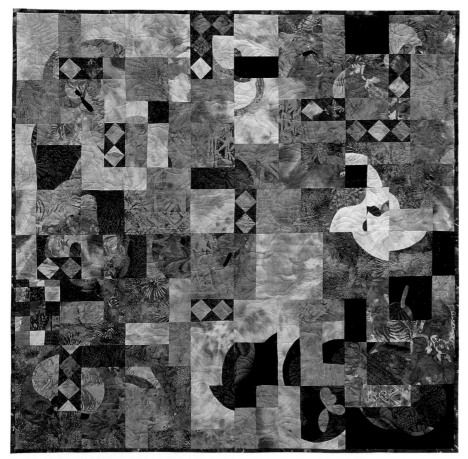

Sunset, Sue Beevers, 2000, 40¹/₂" x 40¹/₂". Hand- and machine-pieced, machine-quilted.

Most people are familiar with a 12-hue color wheel defined by three primary hues: yellow, red, and blue. A **hue** is a specific color, a color name. Hues are fully saturated; they contain as much color as is possible. A **primary** hue is a pure, completely intense color that cannot be mixed from other colors.

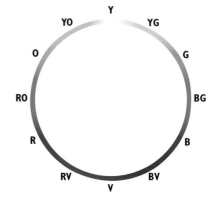

Primary Hues. The fabric is a monoprint.

The three primary hues can be mixed in theoretically equal amounts to form **secondary** colors:

Yellow + red = orange
Red + blue = violet
Blue + yellow = green

Another way to think about this is that each secondary color is halfway between two primaries. Here is where theory and practical application part ways. In reality, only violet can be mixed by using exactly equal amounts of red and blue. It is necessary to use a bit more yellow to create an orange that is halfway between red and yellow. Even more yellow is needed to get a perfect green.

Primary and secondary colors can be mixed in theoretically equal amounts to form **intermediate** colors. An intermediate color is named for the primary color and the secondary color from which it is composed:

Yellow + orange = yellow-orange
Red + orange = red-orange
Red + violet = red-violet
Blue + violet = blue-violet
Blue + green = blue-green
Yellow + green = yellow-green

VALUE

The lightness or darkness of a color is referred to as **value**. Traditionally, the hue with the highest natural value (yellow) is placed at the top of the color wheel and the hue with the lowest natural value (violet) is at the bottom. The hues in between these two have greater or lesser value, as determined by their position on the color wheel. As the hue placement nears the top of the wheel, its value increases. Those hues approaching the bottom decrease in value.

A hue that is not fully saturated is called a **tint**. Whereas a hue is a specific, single color, a tint of that hue can be represented by a whole range of colors. Theoretically, this range starts with just a pinch of the hue and continues to the point just short of full saturation.

Tint ———————————————— Hue

When you are working with opaque paint, a tint is made by mixing the hue plus white. The amount of color added to the white determines the saturation level of the tint. When you

are working with transparent paint, a tint is derived by adding water. The more water you add, the lower the color saturation. Adding moisture to the fabric is another way to diffuse the color and lower the saturation.

As the saturation level of a color increases, its value decreases. In other words, the more color, the darker it appears. This is true even for yellow, the hue with the highest natural value.

Hues and tints can be toned. A **tone** is a color plus its complement. It contains a piece of all three primary colors. The naming of a tone is often subjective, as it represents a range of colors. How much can a blue-green be toned before it ceases to be blue-green and becomes something else? Toning a high-value color, such as yellow, lowers its value. Like tints, tones also can range in saturation levels.

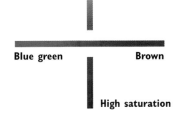

Finally, hues, tints, and tones can be shaded. A **shade** is a color plus black. The term shade refers to the widest range of colors, from those that contain just a touch of black to those that contain a great deal; from those that are fully saturated to those with a low saturation level. The amount of black in a shade can be plotted on a gray scale. When I am painting, I seldom add black to a color because I prefer colors that aren't grayed. If you use black, start with a very small amount. A little bit goes a long, long way.

Tints, Tones, and Shades. A bound resist technique was used.

COLOR HARMONIES

One of the joys of painting fabric is that you can create something that isn't available commercially. As a painter, you can control the colors that you use. Colors can be combined at random or in specific arrangements derived from the color wheel. These arrangements are called **color harmonies**.

A **monochromatic** color harmony is made up of tints, tones, and shades of the same hue. In practical terms, this means that you will start with a single base color. This color will be altered by the addition of water or white paint, a tiny portion of its complement, or just a pinch of black.

An **analogous** color harmony is composed of three adjacent colors on a color wheel. There are twelve different analogous color harmonies possible on a 12-hue color wheel; each color gets to appear in three different combinations. Analogous color harmonies are particularly easy to work with when painting fabric, because color mudding is seldom a problem. Don't forget that each color can be used in different forms: tinted, toned, shaded, or fully intense.

A **complementary** color harmony is formed by two opposite colors on the color wheel. There are six complementary combinations on a 12-hue color wheel. Be careful when painting a complementary color harmony on fabric. A toned color will occur where wet complementary colors meet and mix. Your colors will become muddy if they mix too much. To avoid paint migration, use medium to thick paint and dry or slightly damp fabric. If you don't want the colors to mix at all, spot-dry a section before introducing the complementary color. Remember: Dry colors are permanent; they won't move or mix, unless a transparent color overlaps them.

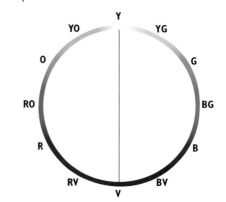

Complementary Color Harmony. Color mixing occurred on the brush and on the wet fabric.

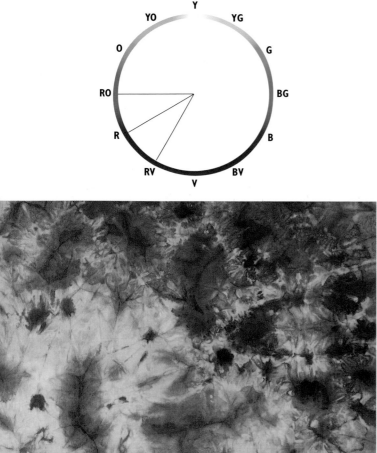

Analogous Colors.
A stitched resist was used.

A **split complementary** color harmony consists of a color plus the two colors on either side of its complement. There are twelve split complementary color harmonies possible on a 12-hue color wheel. Each color can be part of three entirely different split complementary harmonies. This color harmony is very effective on painted fabric. Remember, though, that the colors may tone each other when mixed. The same precautions noted for complementary harmonies apply here.

A **double split complementary** color harmony is a split complementary that goes both ways, for four colors altogether. The colors form a rectangle on the color wheel. There are six different double split complementary color harmonies possible, and each color can be part of two different harmonies. Double splits have the most potential for muddy fabric, since they use colors with a high potential for toning each other.

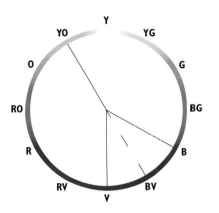

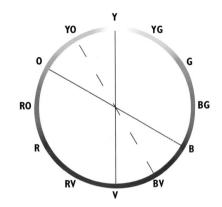

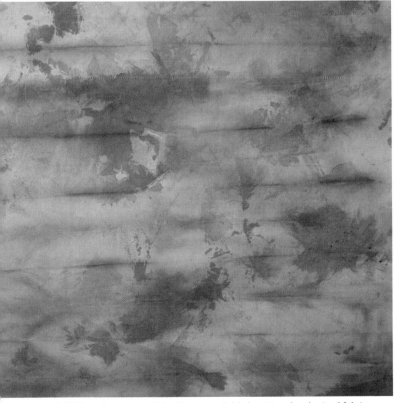

Split Complementary Color Harmony. Folded resist on brush-wiped fabric.

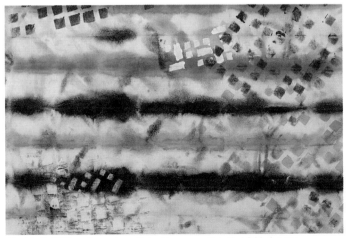

Double Split Complementary Color Harmony. Stenciled folded resist.

■ *People who are new to fabric painting, dyeing, or quilting are often advised to pick their colors from a color wheel. To be honest, this seems a bit impractical to me. Artists seldom work with a palette of pure primary, secondary, and intermediate colors. Instead, they gravitate to the rich diversity and subtlety of tones. Rather than looking for the "perfect" primary hues to start with, I suggest that you make your own version of the color wheel using paint colors that you like or already have.*

A **triadic** color harmony forms an equilateral triangle on the color wheel. There are four triadic color harmonies possible, and each color is part of only one triadic harmony.

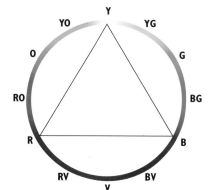

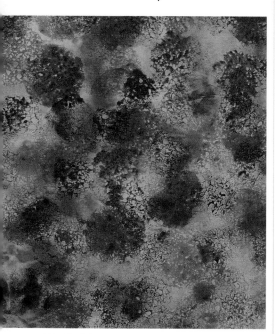

Triadic Color Harmony. *Sponge-stamped fabric.*

There is no reason why you shouldn't make up your own color harmonies. One of my favorites is red-violet, yellow-orange, and blue. No matter what harmony you choose, remember to employ color in varying amounts, saturation levels, and intensities. Follow these principles, take precautions to avoid muddy colors, and you will be successful.

COLOR IN QUILTS

The final step in your color journey is designing a quilt with your hand-painted fabric. Hand-painted fabrics work well by themselves or in combination with commercially printed fabrics. Don't forget that color principles are also at work here.

Sometimes a color will appear to be stronger than its neighbors. This is called **dominance**. Dominance can occur when one color is used a great deal more than the other colors or when it is a great deal lighter (has a higher value). Dominance can also happen when a fully saturated or fully intense color, such as bright red (a pure hue) is placed with less intense colors, such as pink (a tint), rust (a tone), or navy blue (a shade).

Shimmer indicates a competition for dominance. It occurs when two highly contrasting or fully saturated colors are used in the same amounts. The problem is most apparent with stripes, which seem to vibrate or shimmer before the eyes. To avoid shimmer, change the value of one or both colors, widen the stripes, or alter the color ratio.

Sometimes, you want fabric colors to blend together, rather than stand out. **Blending** occurs when lots and lots of small fabric pieces are sewn together and viewed from a distance. *Weaving Life* uses this technique for the hands and textured background. When you take a step back from the quilt, the individual pieces are no longer evident.

Remember, no color stands alone. Colors always play off one another. The color you see is really the relationship between itself and its surroundings.

Weaving Life, Sue Beevers, 2002, 60" x 64". Hand- and machine-pieced, machine-quilted.

YOUR FABRIC
AND WORK AREA

abrics, brushes, and common household supplies round out the equipment needed to set up your painting workshop. You don't need a large or elaborate studio to create beautiful painted fabric, just a space that is well-organized, comfortable, and convenient for you.

THE RIGHT FABRIC

Fabric paint will work on any type of fabric or fabric blend. It is not necessary to buy fabric specially meant for painting or dyeing. For quiltmaking, I like to paint on white or off-white 100% cotton fabrics. White fabrics give the clearest, brightest colors, while natural or off-white fabrics have a yellow cast that mutes the paint color slightly. Often, I will paint a subtle allover visual texture, with little or no white showing through, and then paint over that texture to create a very dense visual effect. I seldom purchase solid-colored fabrics for painting, as I prefer to work with a mottled rather than a flat color base.

As you consider different cotton fabrics for painting, be aware of the thread count, or density, which in turn will affect the way the fabric holds paint. Generally, a fabric with a higher thread count has fewer spaces between threads: it is denser. Paint applied to a dense fabric surface tends to stay in place, making for crisp stenciled, masked, and printed images. A less dense fabric will allow the paint to migrate more easily. If you think of fabric in terms of paint diffusion, at one end of the scale is a very wet, less dense fabric and at the other end is a very dry, high thread-count fabric.

Any good-quality fabric can be used, but, like all quilters, I have my favorite brands. Muslin is the least dense of the fabrics that I use. I find Springs Rangefinder Muslin to be a very nice quality. It comes in bleached and unbleached forms. I use both. Kona PFD and regular cotton fabrics have a medium density. The colored fabric can be discharged prior to painting, leading to interesting effects. Just remember that the underlying cloth color affects the paint color. Springs Southern Belle, cotton broadcloth with a 200-thread count, is my favorite fabric for painting. It is very dense, takes details such as fine lines very well, and feels good to handle. It comes in both white and off-white. The manufacturer's surface finish prevents the paint from being immediately absorbed, allowing effects that can't be achieved with other fabrics.

Unless a recipe notes otherwise, the techniques in this book will work on a variety of cotton fabrics. I suggest that you experiment with different brands and densities to find fabrics that fit your painting and sewing needs.

PRELAUNDERING

Some manufacturers apply a finish coat to their fabrics. This surface finish gives the fabric a crisper appearance on the bolt and makes ironing easier. But it can also interfere with a paint's ability to adhere to the fibers. Fortunately, these finishes are usually easily removed by laundering.

To determine whether a finish is present, do the "sprinkle test." Dip your hand in water, and flick some droplets onto the fabric. Watch to see if the water:

■ **Is instantly absorbed.** This fabric is fine to use as is.

■ **Takes a very short while to absorb.** Prewashing is an option, depending upon the paint you will use and the desired effect. Washing with regular laundry detergent should be sufficient.

■ **Takes a little longer to absorb.** The fabric should be scoured. The following scouring procedure, suggested by PROchem, has worked well for me: Machine-wash on a regular cycle in very hot (140°F) water with $1/2$ teaspoon Synthrapol and $1/2$ teaspoon PRO Dye Activator. Rinse thoroughly.

■ **Just stands on the fabric surface and doesn't absorb.** I would advise not painting this fabric, or at least testing it first. Paint adherence may be a problem.

Prewashed fabric usually wrinkles as it is dried. (Machine-drying or line drying doesn't seem to make a difference.) I don't iron out these wrinkles prior to painting because I like the loose effect that the wrinkled texture gives. If you do iron your fabric, don't apply spray starch or spray sizing. They can affect the paint adherence.

DRYING

After a fabric is painted, but before it is heat-set, it must be allowed to dry thoroughly. Freshly painted fabric can be hung on a clothesline or drying rack. Damp colors will stay put, but remember that very wet paint will migrate downward and bleed into neighboring colors. If this is not your desired effect, the fabric should be laid flat to dry. A hair dryer is great for spot drying; it is not necessary to use heat. Resist the urge to place wet painted fabric in the dryer. It will leave quite a mess. And never place wet painted fabric in the oven. Finally, remember that Pebeo and Golden paints will sunprint when placed in direct sunlight.

Fabric Hung Vertically. Stripes spritzed with water to encourage diffusion.

PAINTING SURFACES

Any flat surface that can be covered by a plastic garbage bag will work as a painting surface. A 24" x 32" piece of Plexiglas or hardboard makes a relatively lightweight, portable painting surface, perfect for painting fat quarters. It can easily be protected from paint and moisture by slipping it into a plastic bag and taping closed.

Larger pieces of fabric, up to $2^{1}/2$ yards long, can be painted on a 4' x 8' sheet of plywood. Here, too, you will want to enclose the board in plastic so that the wood does not absorb the paint. You don't have to be overly fastidious smoothing out the plastic; wrinkles in the surface create interesting textures as you paint.

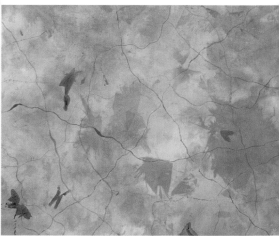

Sponges, brushes, and squeeze bottles created this painted fabric.

My preference is for a hard underlying surface, but some people like to pad their painting boards. This can be easily done by wrapping the board in a large towel before enclosing it in plastic.

EQUIPMENT

The obvious painting tool is, of course, the brush. Brushes come in dozens of sizes and shapes, but it really isn't necessary to have a wide variety. I use three paintbrushes: a #3 outliner (a round watercolor brush with a long, thin, soft bristle), a 1" mop brush (a large round watercolor brush used for background washes), and a 1/2" flat watercolor brush. If you don't have a mop brush, a 1" round sash brush, intended for house painting, can substitute. Foam brushes are good for painting large areas because they hold a lot of paint. They can also be notched with scissors, allowing two or more colors to be applied simultaneously. Even though fabric paint is nontoxic, it is messy. Vinyl, latex, or rubber gloves will protect your hands and prevent paint from being absorbed through your skin.

Moving beyond conventional painting tools expands your creative possibilities. The kitchen in particular is a treasure trove of useful items. Flour, cornstarch, oatmeal, and rice all make successful paste resist. Salt adds a wonderful visual texture to the painted fabric.

Household sponges can be cut in varying widths and shapes for painting or stamping the cloth. Plastic squeeze bottles are perfect for applying squiggly lines of resist or continuous lines of paint. Try ketchup bottles for thicker lines and smaller squeeze bottles for narrow lines. For very fine lines, you'll want to purchase a metal tip applicator bottle, designed especially for painting.

Plastic yogurt or cottage cheese containers will hold water for splashing and fabric dipping. Ice cube trays keep paint colors separate. Small paper cups are good for measuring liquids, but not for holding paint because they start to disintegrate when exposed to moisture over a period of time. Plastic frozen juice containers are great for twisted resist techniques. Mix your paint and resist with plastic spoons or ice cream sticks; spoons can be used for measuring, too.

Other household items can be used in innovative ways. A spray bottle lets me spritz water on a painted surface to encourage diffusion (I don't use it to apply paint). An eyedropper is good for measuring thin liquids, one drop at a time. Plastic packing tape and contact paper make waterproof masking materials. Index cards and file folders are a good thickness for cutting your own stencils. Trowels and putty knives are perfect for spreading resist.

I must admit that I am fascinated with the idea of creating sophisticated fabrics while using rather ordinary items. I'm sure that there are many more fabric painting tools masquerading as ordinary household items that I have overlooked. Someday, when least expected, I will discover them.

■ *Keep food storage and painting equipment separate. Once you have used a container or utensil for paint, **never ever** reuse it for food or eating. If you paint small pieces of fabric on a kitchen counter, be careful to move and cover any food and eating utensils prior to painting.*

SIMPLE FREE-FORM
TECHNIQUES

SPLATTERS
AND SPLASHES

Splattering, splashing, and dribbling are perhaps the simplest and quickest ways to create an exciting piece of fabric. A brush is dipped into the prepared paint and then tapped over a finger, releasing the paint in anywhere from a fine spray to heavy droplets. The brush never touches the fabric surface. The further the brush is held from the fabric, the wider and longer the splatter arc. Splatters are notorious for falling in unexpected places, including surrounding surfaces as well as on the painter, so take adequate precautions. When the brush is held vertically, the splatters generally fall in a more concentrated area.

The size of the brush is an important factor in controlling the amount of splatters and the splatter size. A small brush will give a few small splatters. A large brush will give large splatters.

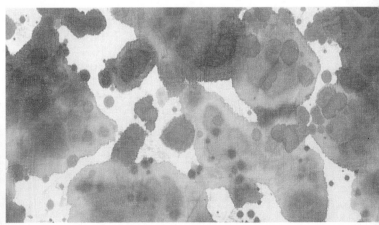

Large and Small Splatters

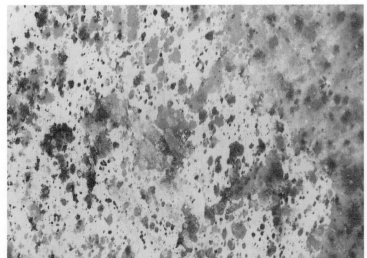

**Brush-Controlled
Splatter Pattern**

There is an exception. A large round brush, lightly dipped into thin paint, will yield a lot of tiny splatters. The amount and consistency of the paint also affects the splatter. More paint will yield larger spots. Thick paint will yield larger, fewer spots.

Fabric moisture also affects splatter size. Splatters will diffuse slightly on spritzed fabric.

Splatters diffuse even more readily on wet fabric. A very interesting effect can be achieved by splashing water on dry fabric prior to splattering. The paint splatter will hold its shape in dry areas and diffuse in wet ones.

Splatters on Water-Splashed Fabric

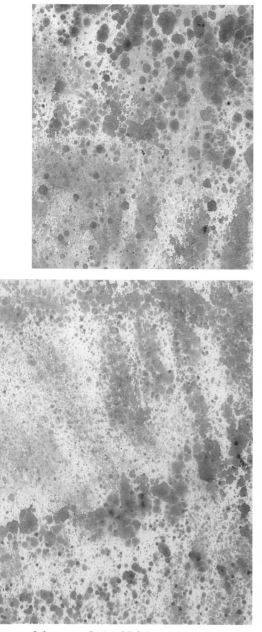

Splatters on Spritzed Fabric

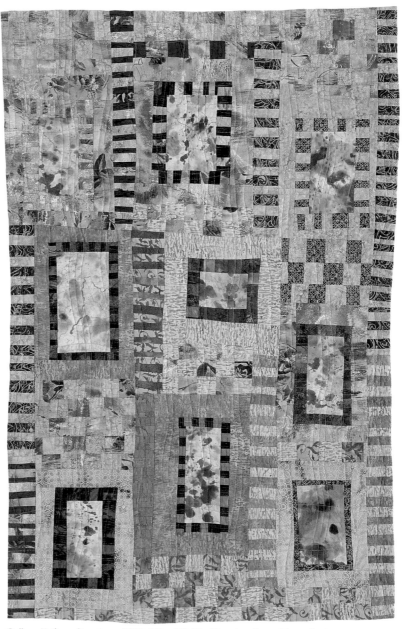

Gallery, Kathryn Stenstrom, 2002, 34" x 54". Machine-pieced, machine-quilted.

Experimenting with splatters can lead to wonderful visual effects. Here are a few suggestions:

■ **FLICKING** Hang the fabric vertically, load the brush with paint, and flick the brush with your wrist. A vertical trail of spots will form. When you spritz the fabric with water, the spots will leave a downward trail.

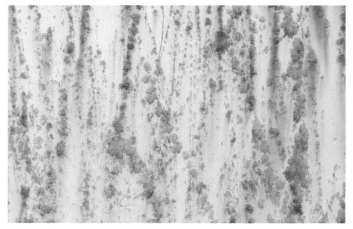

Flicked Splatters

■ **SPLASHING** A large round brush loaded with paint will give huge splashes. Thin paint will form the largest splashes and diffuse more easily than thick paint. Wet fabric will encourage diffusion. A large halo will form around the splash if the fabric is very wet. If you don't want splashed colors to blend, you will need to dry the fabric between color changes.

Splashes on Wet Fabric

■ **SPLASHING, CRUMPLING, AND FOLDING**
Fabric can be splashed with paint and then crumpled or folded, transferring the paint to another portion of the fabric. The fabric can then be opened, and the painting continued.

Splashed, Crumpled, Folded

■ **DRIBBLING** Springs Southern Belle natural-colored cotton broadcloth has a light finish that prevents paint from being immediately absorbed. If this unwashed fabric is splattered with paint, hung vertically, and lightly spritzed with water, the surface finish allows the paint to roll downward before being absorbed. Note that you must work very quickly. If the paint dries or gets absorbed before the hanging and spritzing steps, it won't dribble.

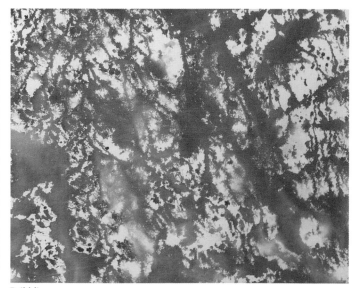

Dribbling

SPRINKLES

Fine paint sprinkles can create overall surface texture or they can be applied in selected areas for an interesting finishing touch.

Prepare your color palette:

- violet ■ blue ■ yellow-orange
Make all a thin consistency.

YOU'LL ALSO NEED:

- Springs Southern Belle cotton broadcloth (do not prewash)
- water-filled spray bottle
- 1" mop brush

1. Lay the fabric flat. Spritz lightly with water.

2. Lightly dip a 1" mop brush in violet paint. Don't overload the brush, or large blotches will form. Gently splatter the surface of the fabric. Aim for an overall effect, instead of concentrating the color in one area. Reload the brush as needed. Rinse the brush thoroughly when you are through.

3. Repeat Step 2 using blue paint. The splattered colors will overlap naturally. The amount of color used is up to you. (Blue dominates in the sample fabric.)

4. Repeat Step 2 using yellow-orange paint.

5. Lightly spritz the fabric in selected areas to encourage color diffusion.

6. Lay the fabric flat to dry.

FABRIC TIP: THIS RECIPE TAKES ADVANTAGE OF THE MANUFACTURER'S SURFACE FINISH ON SPRINGS SOUTHERN BELLE COTTON BROADCLOTH. THE FINISH ACTS AS A SHIELD, SO THAT WET PAINT TAKES LONGER TO PENETRATE. THE PAINT DRIES BEFORE IT DIFFUSES, RESULTING IN TINY SPRINKLES OF COLOR.

SPLASHES

Wet fabric and thin paint encourage splashes of paint to diffuse and blend.

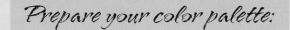

Prepare your color palette:

- yellow - red-violet - blue-violet

Use Golden Fluid Acrylic paints. Thin with water (use a 4:1 water-to-paint ratio) and a few drops of GAC 900.

YOU'LL ALSO NEED:
- fabric
- 1" mop brush
- 1" flat watercolor brush
- water-filled spray bottle

1. Lay the fabric flat. Use a 1" mop brush to splash clear water over the surface.

2. Dip the 1" mop brush into the yellow paint. Without wiping off the excess, immediately splash the paint onto the wet fabric. Rinse the brush thoroughly when you are through. Spritz the fabric surface with clear water to encourage diffusion. Allow the fabric to dry until it is just slightly damp.

3. Repeat Step 2 using red-violet paint.

4. Repeat Step 2 using blue-violet paint.

5. Dip a 1" flat watercolor brush into very thin red-violet paint and lightly splatter the fabric. Rinse the brush.

Repeat using very thin blue-violet paint. Spritz the surface with water to encourage diffusion.

6. Lay the fabric flat to dry.

PAINTBOX TIP: FOR A WATERY APPEARANCE, GOLDEN FLUID ACRYLIC IS IDEAL. THE PIGMENTS CAN FLOAT A GREAT DEAL OF WATER WITHOUT SEPARATING. ADDING GAC 900 TO THE PAINT EXTENDS THE OPEN TIME FOR BETTER COLOR BLENDING.

LINES

Free-form lines, squiggles, and swirls make for interesting painted effects. Use them alone or in conjunction with other techniques. A gently curving fine line, a small fine squiggle, or even some fine short strokes can often add the perfect finishing touch to a fabric.

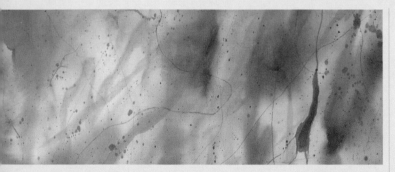

Lines as a Finishing Touch

The size of the brush determines the width of the line formed on the fabric: the smaller the brush, the finer the line. Turning a flat brush as the line is painted will vary the width.

Any paint will work, but for the clearest line definition, use a very dense fabric. A thick paint will give a clean, well-defined edge. It is most easily applied on a slightly damp fabric. Thin paint, because it has a tendency to diffuse easily, gives a softer edge. The edge will soften further on wet fabric.

As you explore lines, concentrate on enjoying the physical motion and the materials, not on creating a realistic image of a specific object. Experiment with brush stroke variations. Enjoy the color blending.

Lines from a Flat Brush

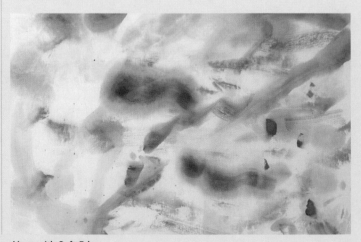

Lines with Soft Edge

■ **HATCHING** Hatches, or single directional lines, and crosshatches are drawing techniques traditionally used for shading. They can also create a distinctive fabric, particularly when used in small areas. Add them with a fine outliner brush or a metal tip applicator bottle.

Brushed Hatching

■ **MORE THAN ONE COLOR** Each corner of a notched foam brush, a flat brush, or a household sponge can be dipped into a different color paint and then used to apply two or more colors simultaneously. The colors will blend slightly where they meet, especially if the fabric is wet. If you are using complementary colors, rinse the brush or sponge before reloading to avoid a muddy mix.

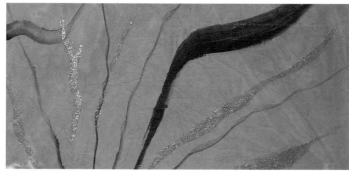

Using Two Colors

■ **SQUEEZE BOTTLES** For very fine lines, use a medium to heavy viscosity paint in a metal tip applicator bottle. For a thicker line, use a regular tapered-tip bottle, such as a ketchup bottle. Spritz with water to encourage diffusion.

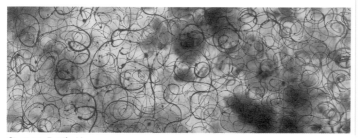

Squeeze Bottle Line

■ **STRIPES AND PLAIDS** Stripes do not have to be straight or perfectly horizontal or vertical in orientation. They can wave or zigzag across the fabric. Paint some horizontal stripes, hang the fabric vertically, and spritz with water. Gravity will do the rest—the wet stripes will bleed into each other. Use a combination of vertical and horizontal stripes to make a plaid. The stripes don't have to extend across the entire fabric, be completely straight, or have the same color order. Just the suggestion of a plaid creates a very interesting fabric.

Drippy Stripes

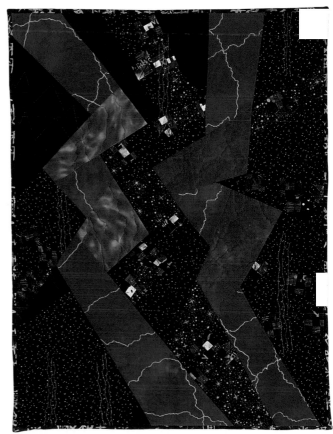

Northern Lightning, Gail Strout, 2002, 22½" x 29½". Machine-pieced, machine-quilted.

LINES AND **SPLATTERS**

Opaque paint splatters overlay new colors on this dipped fabric. Fine lines add a crosshatched texture.

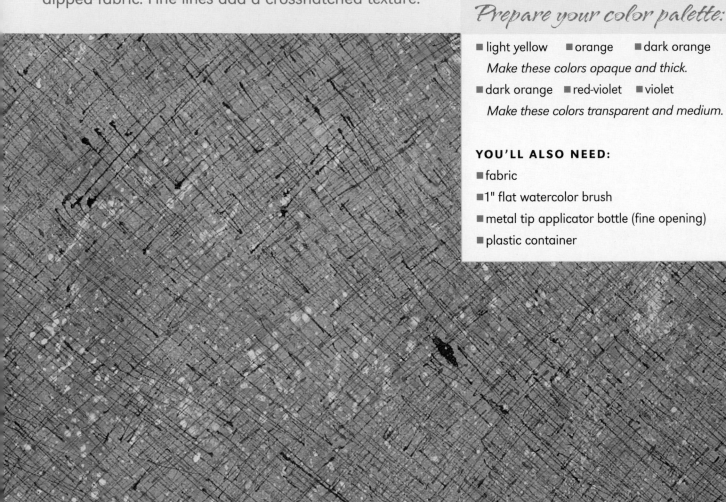

Prepare your color palette:

- light yellow   ■ orange   ■ dark orange

Make these colors opaque and thick.

- dark orange   ■ red-violet   ■ violet

Make these colors transparent and medium.

YOU'LL ALSO NEED:

- fabric
- 1" flat watercolor brush
- metal tip applicator bottle (fine opening)
- plastic container

1. Fill a plastic container partway with water. Add a few drops of dark orange transparent paint and stir. Dip the fabric into the container long enough to wet and tint it, and then remove it. Allow the fabric to dry thoroughly.

2. Use a 1" flat watercolor brush to splatter opaque paint on the fabric, first light yellow, then orange, and finally dark orange. It is not necessary to clean the brush between color changes. Lay the fabric flat to dry.

3. Fill a metal tip applicator bottle with red-violet paint. Randomly "draw" fine lines in a loose zigzag pattern across the fabric, maintaining a diagonal orientation.

4. Turn the fabric 90°. Repeat Step 3 with violet paint, making the new zigzags cross the previous ones at a right angle.

Thoroughly rinse the applicator tip after each use to prevent clogging.

5. Lay the fabric flat to dry.

PAINTBOX TIP: SPLATTERS OF MEDIUM TO THICK OPAQUE PAINT WILL HOLD THEIR SHAPE, INSTEAD OF BLENDING TOGETHER AND FORMING A NEW COLOR. THICKER SPLATTERS TAKE LONGER TO DRY, AND A PRESSING CLOTH IS NEEDED TO IRON THE FINISHED FABRIC.

MOSTLY **PLAID**

A brush is lightly stroked through wet splatters to create this plaid effect.

Prepare your color palette:

- blue-green ■ violet ■ dark blue-violet
Make all a thin consistency.

YOU'LL ALSO NEED:
- natural Springs Southern Belle cotton broadcloth (do not prewash)
- 1" mop brush ■ foam brush
- water-filled spray bottle
- Pebeo Gold Glitter Finish

1. Lay the fabric flat. Spritz lightly with water.

2. Use a 1" mop brush to lightly splatter blue-green paint onto the fabric. Immediately rinse and dry the brush so that the bristles are fluffy and separated.

3. Touch the bristles *very lightly* to the fabric surface and draw them through the wet paint droplets to make thin horizontal lines. Clean the brush as needed. The combination of dry, fluffy bristles and a light touch produces the thinnest lines.

4. Turn the fabric 90° and repeat Step 3. The lines will cross at right angles, for a plaid effect.

5. Spritz selected areas with water to encourage the brushed lines to bleed. Allow the fabric to partially dry.

6. Repeat Steps 2–5 using violet and then dark violet paint. Keep in mind that the color you use the most will dominate.

7. Lay the fabric flat and let it dry thoroughly. Then use a foam brush to apply Gold Glitter Finish.

DESIGN TIP: DON'T OVERDO THE BRUSH STROKES OR TRY TO MAKE THE LINES EXACTLY PARALLEL AND PERPENDICULAR. JUST THE SUGGESTION OF A PLAID IS WHAT MAKES THIS FABRIC INTERESTING.

WIPEOUT

Accent colors wiped off an ice cream stick
jazz up this fabric.

Prepare your color palette:

- blue-green (thin) ■ blue (thin)
- several accent colors (thick)
- orange (medium to thin)

   Make various consistencies, as noted.

YOU'LL ALSO NEED:
- fabric ■ 1" mop brush
- #3 watercolor outliner brush
- ice cream stick

1. Lay the fabric flat. Use a 1" mop brush to randomly splash clear water on the surface. Allow some areas to be wet, some damp, and some dry. Crumple the fabric.

2. Dip the 1" mop brush in water and then in blue-green paint. Wipe the brush with the crumpled fabric. Recrumple the fabric and repeat the dipping and wiping process a few more times. The paint will diffuse and lighten as it touches the wet areas of the fabric. Repeat with blue paint. Lay the fabric flat and let it dry thoroughly.

3. Dip an ice cream stick into an accent color. Wipe the stick with the fabric. Repeat with the same or a different accent color as desired. Let dry thoroughly.

4. Dip a #3 watercolor outliner brush into orange paint. Draw the brush across the surface to paint fine lines.

5. Lay the fabric flat to dry.

⊕ TOOL TIP: A FINE OUTLINER BRUSH HOLDS A SURPRISINGLY LARGE AMOUNT OF PAINT. MORE PAINT MEANS THICKER LINES. AS THE AMOUNT OF PAINT ON THE BRUSH DIMINISHES, THE LINES BECOME FINER.

TOTAL **WIPEOUT**

Tiny paint splatters add interest to this brush-wiped fabric.

Prepare your color palette:

- navy blue (thin)
- dark blue-violet (medium)
  Make two consistencies, as noted.

YOU'LL ALSO NEED:

- natural Springs Southern Belle cotton broadcloth (do not prewash)
- 1" mop brush
- water-filled spray bottle

1. Lay the fabric flat. Lightly dip a 1" mop brush into navy blue paint. Gently splatter the paint across the surface of the fabric. Spritz lightly with water, just enough to encourage some diffusion. Let dry thoroughly.
2. Gently crumple the fabric. Dip the mop brush into dark blue-violet paint. Wipe the brush in the fabric folds. Repeat the crumpling, dipping, and wiping sequence one more time.
3. Immediately dip the same brush in water. Wipe the brush in the fabric. Lay the fabric flat to dry.

PAINTBOX TIP: WHEN YOU MIX NAVY AND VIOLET PAINT TOGETHER TO MAKE BLUE-VIOLET, DON'T OVERDO IT. A LESS-THAN-THOROUGH MIXING WILL ALLOW THE VIOLET PIGMENT TO STAND OUT WHEN THE FABRIC IS SPRITZED. THIS EFFECT OCCURS BECAUSE VIOLET DIFFUSES MORE QUICKLY THAN NAVY BLUE.

BACKGROUND
TEXTURES

BASIC VISUAL TEXTURES

Use each of these easy techniques on its own or to make a background texture for other paint applications. When a colored background is desired, but commercially available solid-colored fabrics are too plain, the methods described here can help you bridge the gap.

■ BRUSHING ON A TEXTURED SURFACE

Place a dry or slightly damp fabric on a textured surface, and the painting will pick up the characteristic texture. A wrinkled plastic bag makes a wonderful textured painting surface—and it's waterproof. Flat objects like buttons, feathers, and cardboard cutouts can be placed underneath the fabric for additional design interest.

Spritzed and Wiped

Plastic Bag Texture

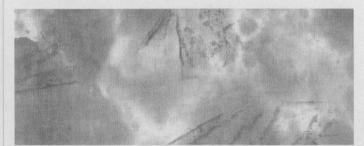

Wiped, Spritzed, Wiped

■ FABRIC WIPING
This technique lets you mop up wet paint that's left behind on the painting surface. Paint seepage is most likely when the fabric is wet, the thread count is low (such as in muslin), or the paint is thin. Just wad up a fresh piece of fabric into a wrinkled ball and use it to wipe the surface clean.

If all of the paint isn't picked up in the first pass, spritz a bit of water on the surface and repeat the process.

Dusk, Sue Beevers, 2000, 40" x 40". Hand- and machine-pieced, machine-quilted.

■ **FABRIC STAMPING** In this technique, a piece of fabric is wadded up, dipped in paint, and then used to stamp another fabric. The process can be repeated with the same or a different color. The folds in the fabric wad become permanently stamped on the fabric surface.

The amount of moisture in the "stamper" fabric is an important consideration. If the fabric is dry or only damp, the paint will not penetrate to the fabric layers under the fold. Spritzing the stamped fabric with clear water will encourage the paint to diffuse.

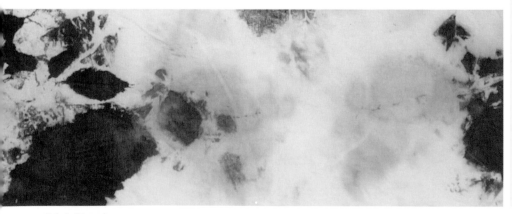

Fabric Stamping

■ **SECOND-GENERATION FABRICS I** One painted fabric can be used to paint another by layering the two together prior to painting. The lower, second-generation fabric will absorb any excess paint from the top fabric as it is being painted. Key principles to remember: Thin paint migrates more easily than a thicker paint, paint seeps more easily through less dense weaves, and a damp or wet upper fabric encourages the paint to diffuse outward and migrate downward.

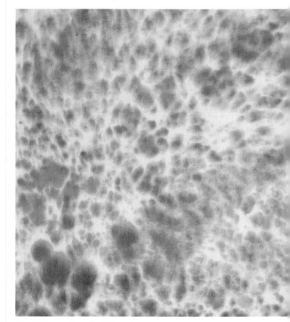

First Generation Splatters I

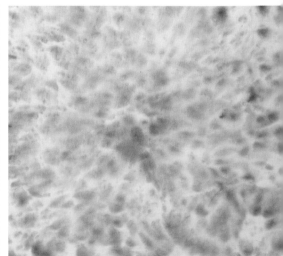

Second Generation Splatters I

■ SECOND-GENERATION FABRICS II

Another way to create a second-generation fabric is to paint one fabric, place another fabric on top, and go over them with a roller. The more you roll, the more the paint will transfer. The result depends on the amount and dampness of the paint on the first fabric and the dampness of the second fabric. The first fabric will always become lighter than it was originally, as paint is transferred to the second.

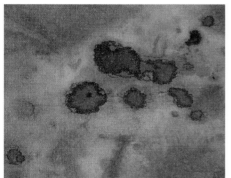 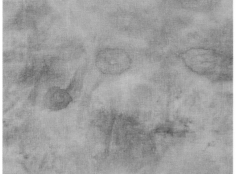

First Generation Splatters II   Second Generation Splatters II

■ FABRIC DIPPING

To give fabric a light tint, dip it into the water used to clean paintbrushes. If a more saturated color is desired, start with a fresh container of water and add a few drops of paint. Variables in this method are the amount of water, the size of the container, and the amount of paint. A large container lets you swish the fabric around, so that the suspended color can reach all parts. A smaller container inhibits movement, so that some parts of the fabric may not get painted.

■ COLOR GRADATION SERIES

This dipping method allows you to create progressively lighter colors in a series of fabrics. Dip the first fabric, squeeze out the excess moisture, and set it out to dry. Add a little water to the remaining color, dip a second fabric, and set it out to dry. The color in the second piece will be less saturated than the first. Repeat the process until the color has been exhausted. For a graded color series, use fat quarters and return 2 tablespoons of water to the container after each dip.

First Dipping

Second Dipping

■ COLOR MOVEMENT SERIES

This dipping method lets you move from one color to another color in incremental steps. Start with any desired color. Dip the first fabric, squeeze out the excess moisture, and set it out to dry. Add 2 tablespoons of water plus a few drops of the new color. Dip the second fabric, squeeze out the excess moisture, and set it out to dry. Continue adding water and a few drops of the new color after each dip until the fabric color ceases to change. Color movement fabrics are quite wrinkled due to wringing. The wrinkles will sunprint if Pebeo or Golden Acrylic paint is used.

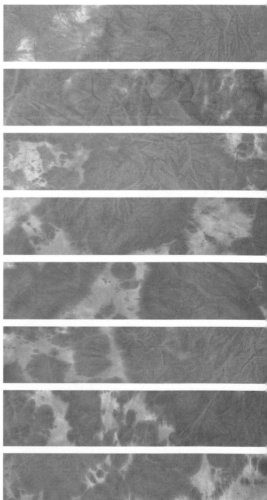

Color Movement in 8 Stages

FABRIC **STAMPING**

This fabric was created by stamping on a surface covered by a wrinkled plastic bag. The technique combines a textured work surface, crumpled cloth, and splattered paint.

Prepare your color palette:

- green
- blue-violet
- red-violet
- yellow-orange

  Make all a thin consistency.

YOU'LL ALSO NEED:

- fabric
- 1" mop brush
- water-filled spray bottle
- large plastic bag

1. Crumple the plastic bag, smooth it out over a flat painting surface, and tape down the edges. Note that the bag must be larger than the fabrics to be painted.

2. Use the plastic-covered work surface for various fabric painting recipes. As you finish painting a fabric, set it aside for drying. Immediately crumple your "stamping" fabric and wipe it across the wet plastic to pick up the remaining paint residue. Lay the "stamping" fabric flat and spritz lightly to encourage diffusion. Allow to dry, either partially or thoroughly as desired. Repeat the stamping process over the course of various projects to pick up as many different colors as you wish.

3. Use a 1" mop brush to lightly splatter green, blue-violet, red-violet, and yellow-orange paint on the crumpled plastic work surface. Crumple the fabric and stamp it onto the surface to pick up the various colors. Rearrange the crumples and stamp again. Repeat until all the paint is absorbed. Lay the fabric flat to dry.

STUDIO TIP: GET IN THE HABIT OF USING A PIECE OF FABRIC TO CLEAN YOUR WORK SURFACE AFTER PAINTING. THIS WIPING CLOTH CAN THEN BECOME A BASE FABRIC FOR OTHER TECHNIQUES.

CONFINED COLOR DRIBBLING

Try this technique on both dry and wet
fabrics for two different effects.

Prepare your color palette:

- blue ■red ■yellow
Make all a thin consistency.

YOU'LL ALSO NEED:

- 1 fat quarter (18" x 22" piece of fabric)
- measuring spoons
- zip-close plastic sandwich bag

Dry

Wet

1. Bunch up a dry or damp fat quarter and place it in a plastic bag. Do not compress the fabric.

2. Use a measuring spoon to dribble blue paint over the fabric. Repeat with the red and yellow paints. You'll need about 9 teaspoons total to color a dry fat quarter, 3 teaspoons for a damp fat quarter. The color that is used most tends to dominate. The color that is added last will blend less than the one that is added first.

3. Seal the bag, squeezing out as much excess air as possible. Let sit for at least 20 minutes, or until paint droplets are no longer visible inside the bag. To accelerate the process, place the bag in the sunlight and watch for clear condensation to form. As the fabric absorbs the paint, the colors will diffuse and migrate, forming secondary colors.

4. Remove the fabric from the bag and unfold it. Lay the fabric flat or hang to dry.

FABRIC TIP: TRY NOT TO CONCENTRATE THE COLOR DRIBBLING IN ONE AREA OF THE FABRIC. THE COLORS WILL APPEAR DARKER ON DRY FABRIC, LIGHTER ON DAMP FABRIC. DAMP FABRIC WILL PROMOTE COLOR MIGRATION.

SALTING

Sprinkling salt on wet painted fabric creates a unique effect. Salt attracts and absorbs the moisture in the paint. The paint particles suspended in the water also move toward the salt, leaving behind a light streak or halo. The color concentrates in a deposit under the salt crystal.

Salt Streaking

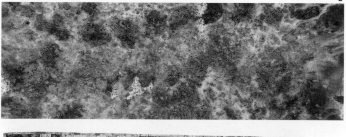

Five factors determine the visual outcome of this technique: atmospheric moisture, paint viscosity, fabric moisture, salt particle size, and amount of salt used. Salting works best on a dry, sunny day, because the fabric moisture isn't competing with the air moisture. Thin paint works better than thick paint because it diffuses more easily. It also helps if the painted fabric is very damp or wet. More moisture allows the suspended paint to flow more easily. Be careful, though. If the fabric is too wet, the salt particles may dissolve. Any salt can be used, even table salt. A large particle will leave a larger light streak than a smaller particle. Halite, or snow melt, is a large particle and best at attracting and absorbing water.

More salt means more streaks. Salt sprinkled in a concentrated place will create a mottled effect.

Mottling

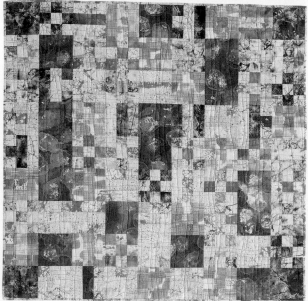

Halite

Watermarks, Kathryn Stenstrom, 2002, 40" x 40". Machine-pieced, machine-quilted.

FIREWORKS

Large halite particles, combined with water-spritzed paint sprinkles, create bursts of color.

Prepare your color palette:

- yellow-green ■ red-violet ■ blue-violet
- *Make all a thin consistency.*

YOU'LL ALSO NEED:
- white fabric
- halite (salt particles)
- 1" mop brush
- water-filled spray bottle

1. Lay the fabric flat. Spritz lightly with clear water. Let the fabric sit a few minutes so that the water is fully absorbed.

2. Use a 1" mop brush to splatter yellow-green paint across the surface. Rinse the brush thoroughly. Splatter red-violet paint and blue-violet paint in the same way, rinsing between color changes. Work quickly, as this technique relies on the migration of wet paint.

3. Place the fabric outdoors in the sunlight. Spritz the fabric thoroughly with water, to encourage the splattered colors to blend.

4. Sprinkle halite over the wet surface. Let the fabric dry completely. Brush off the halite particles and save them for future use.

DESIGN TIP: TRY NOT TO CONCENTRATE THE HALITE PARTICLES IN ONE AREA. THE VISUAL EFFECT IS MUCH MORE STRIKING WHEN THEY DON'T OVERLAP EACH OTHER.

TRIO

Variations in the salt particle size create exciting visual texture.

Prepare your color palette:

- blue ■ violet ■ yellow-orange ■ red-violet
Make all a thin consistency.

YOU'LL ALSO NEED:
- fabric
- mixture of sea salt, table salt, and halite
- 1" mop brush
- water-filled spray bottle

1. Wet the fabric thoroughly and lay it flat.

2. Dip a 1" mop brush into blue paint. Splash the paint onto the fabric. As the paint diminishes on the brush, spritz the bristles lightly with water and continue splashing the fabric. Continue spritzing the bristles and splashing the fabric until all the paint on the brush is exhausted. Rinse the brush thoroughly.

3. Repeat Step 2 with the violet, and then the yellow-orange and red-violet paints. Remember to rinse the brush thoroughly between color changes.

4. Place the fabric outdoors in the sunlight. Spritz the fabric surface with water to encourage color blending and diffusion.

5. Sprinkle the 3 different salts across the surface. Let the fabric dry completely. Brush off the salt particles and save them for reuse.

STUDIO TIP: SUCCESS WITH SALT TECHNIQUES DEPENDS LARGELY ON THE AIR HUMIDITY. DRY AIR IS OPTIMAL; MOIST, HUMID AIR IS NOT. SALT TECHNIQUES ARE POSSIBLE IN SOME INDOOR ENVIRONMENTS, SUCH AS DRY HEATED AIR THAT MANY HOMES EXPERIENCE IN WINTER.

SUNPRINTING

Sunprinting is simple: Lay wet, painted fabric in direct sunlight, place flat objects such as washers, leaves, or cardboard cutouts on top, and allow the fabric to dry. Each spot on the fabric that was masked off will be lighter, leaving an imprint of the mask on the surface. The effect is most pronounced when very saturated colors are used.

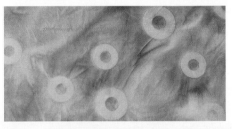

Washers and Wrinkles

Not every paint will sunprint. I recommend Golden Fluid Acrylic (especially the more transparent colors and colors containing blue) and Pebeo transparent paints. Of the two, Pebeo prints the most readily.

Sunprinting works best on hot, dry, cloudless days. These conditions encourage the fabric to dry quickly. If you want a clearly defined edge, choose a very flat object for printing. A thicker object will cast a shadow, creating a blurred edge. To encourage blurring, remove the masking object before the paint is completely dry and spritz the fabric surface.

Clearly Defined Edge

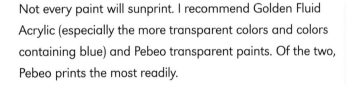

Sunprinted Wrinkles

Wrinkles in the fabric will also sunprint. The effect is visually very interesting and can be exploited. Fabric painted by dipping or color dribbling emerges from the process quite wrinkled. The tiny sunprinted wrinkles make a wonderful background for other painting techniques.

Don't forget that flat objects can be placed on wet wrinkled fabric. How clearly the edges sunprint depends upon where they fall on the wrinkle.

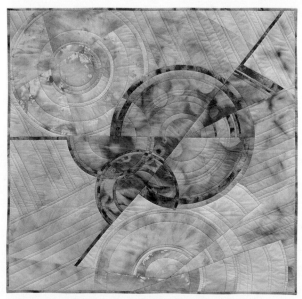

Geometric Construction with Bi, Sue Beevers, 2001, 41" x 41". Hand- and machine-pieced, machine-quilted.

FERN **SHADOWS**

Assorted ferns were sunprinted on a sunny,
cloudless day in the early afternoon.

Prepare your color palette:

- red-violet - dark-blue - green

*Use Pebeo Setacolor Textile paints. Thin with
water (use a 2:1 water-to-paint ratio).*

YOU'LL ALSO NEED:
- fabric - ferns - foam brush
- water-filled spray bottle
- portable plastic-wrapped board

1. Lay the fabric flat on a portable board. Spritz the fabric surface thoroughly with water. Let sit a few minutes, or until the fabric absorbs the moisture completely.

2. Use a foam brush to apply green paint to small areas of the fabric. Apply the red-violet and dark blue paints in the same way, rinsing the brush between colors. Work quickly, so that the paint doesn't dry.

3. Move the fabric outdoors to a sunny location. Arrange several ferns on top. Leave them in place until the fabric is dry. In the sample fabric, fronds that rested flat against the fabric printed sharp and clear, while fronds that curved up and away from the surface were blurred and shadowy.

The overall effect is of ferns fading in and out of focus. Spritzing selected areas will also increase the blurring by allowing the wet paint to diffuse a bit more.

TOOL TIP: SOME LEAVES AND FERNS SHRIVEL PRETTY QUICKLY AFTER THEY ARE PICKED. THIS IS ESPECIALLY TRUE ON HOT, DRY SUNNY DAYS. PLACE YOUR SPECIMENS IN A JAR OF COOL WATER AND SET IT IN THE SHADE UNTIL YOU ARE READY FOR THEM.

SUNPRINT

Organic and inorganic objects combine in this sunprinted fabric. Use thin leaves to print crisp edges. Use thick, spongy leaves for softer, fuzzier edges and a shadowy appearance.

Prepare your color palette:

- yellow-orange ■ violet ■ red-violet

Use Pebeo Setacolor Textile paints. Make all a thin consistency.

YOU'LL ALSO NEED:

- fabric ■ leaves
- 2" foam brush ■ 1" mop brush
- galvanized washers, 1/2" to 1 3/4" diameter
- portable plastic-wrapped board

1. Wet the fabric thoroughly and lay it on a portable board.

2. Use a 2" foam brush to apply yellow-orange paint to the fabric in selected areas. Rinse the brush thoroughly. Apply violet paint in the same way. Use a 1" mop brush to splatter a few drops of red-violet paint onto the surface.

3. Move the fabric outdoors to a sunny location. Gently bunch up the fabric with your fingers, for a crinkled surface. Place the washers on the crinkled fabric at random. Let sit about 5 minutes, or until the fabric is damp but no longer sopping.

4. Straighten out the fabric without disturbing the washer placement. Place leaves on the fabric surface. Let dry.

STUDIO TIP: IF YOU LIVE IN SNOW COUNTRY LIKE I DO, YOU CAN STILL SUNPRINT IN THE WINTER. LAY THE WET FABRIC INDOORS IN A SUN PATCH. THIS WORKS BEST IN MID TO LATE WINTER, WHEN YOUR HOUSE IS THE DRIEST.

PRINT
TECHNIQUES

SPONGE
STAMPING

ny kind of sponge can stamp fabric, but I prefer the texture of natural or cellulose household sponges to those made of foam. The stamped effect depends on the amount of moisture in both fabric and paint, the amount of paint on the sponge, and the pressure you apply when stamping.

A thick paint, brushed onto the sponge, works best for sponge stamping. Simply press the loaded sponge onto the fabric. The first "stamp" will release a lot of paint, the next, a bit less, and the next even less, so you'll need to replenish the paint fairly often. Resist the urge to overload the sponge; the spongy texture is most evident if very little paint is used.

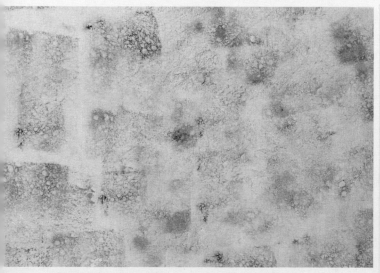

Household Sponge Texture

Heavy to Light Stamps

You can create interesting effects by loading more than one paint color on the sponge at a time. Once again, loading is most neatly and easily done with a brush. Remember that the colors will blend, especially if the sponge has been predampened with water.

For a different look, stamp a geometric grid pattern first and then superimpose some free-form stamps wherever you like. "Ignoring" the grid positioning for the extra stamps will lead to a dynamic, visually interesting piece.

after each stamp. The stamped motifs will have clean, hard edges at first and will progressively lose their shape as the moisture in the sponge increases. Don't forget that water can be spritzed onto the fabric after stamping, to encourage diffusion.

Stamping with Two Colors

Combination Grid and Free-Form

Spritzing the Sponge

Cellulose sponges come in various geometric shapes—squares, rectangles, circles, and ovals—that lend themselves to free-form fabric design. If you can't find a particular shape, you can cut your own with scissors. Turning the sponge a bit each time you stamp adds a nice variation to the stamped design. Try combining different shapes and sizes on the same fabric.

For well-defined shapes, stamp on dry or lightly spritzed fabric. For a gradual diffusion, spritz the sponge with water

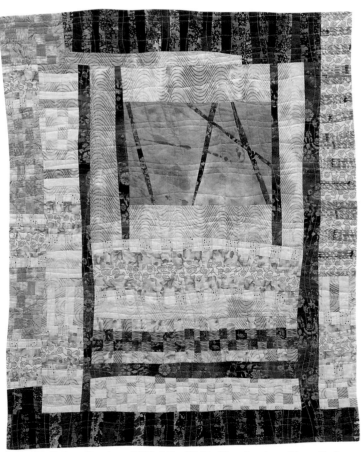

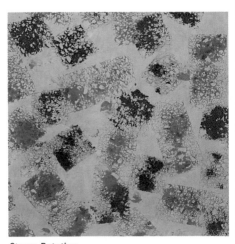

Stamp Rotation

Reflection, Kathryn Stenstrom, 2002, 34" x 42". Machine-pieced, machine-quilted.

A WRINKLE **IN TIME**

A lightly painted household sponge leaves behind a lovely stamped texture.

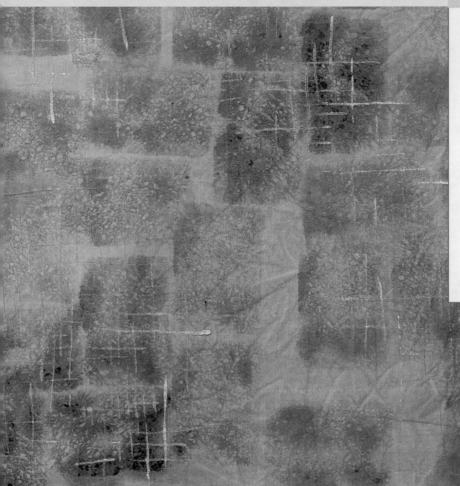

Prepare your color palette:

- anthroquinone blue
- quinacridone gold and interference gold, mixed 1:1

Use Golden Fluid Acrylic paints. Use as is (a medium consistency).

YOU'LL ALSO NEED:
- fabric
- Silk Screen Fabric Gel
- 1" flat watercolor brush
- metal tip applicator bottle (fine opening)
- 2" x 3" household sponge
- water-filled spray bottle
- plastic container

1. Fill a plastic container with 1 cup of water. Add a few drops of anthroquinone blue. Dunk the crumpled fabric into the solution and swish around to color all areas. Remove the fabric and wring out the excess moisture. Do not smooth out the wrinkles. Lay the fabric outdoors in the sunlight to dry. The wrinkles will sunprint.

2. Lay the dry sunprinted fabric flat. Spritz with water. Also dampen the sponge.

3. Mix anthroquinone blue and the silk screen fabric gel in a 1:1 ratio. Brush a thin coating of the thickened paint onto the sponge. Stamp the sponge onto the damp fabric, maintaining a general vertical/horizontal orientation. As the paint in the sponge is used up, spritz it lightly with water and continue stamping until the paint is exhausted. Reapply paint as necessary. Let the fabric dry thoroughly.

4. Use a metal tip applicator bottle to apply the mixed gold paint in a cross-hatching design. Let dry.

TOOL TIP: TO MAKE A VERY FINE, UNINTERRUPTED LINE, APPLY MEDIUM CONSISTENCY PAINT USING A METAL TIP APPLICATOR BOTTLE.

CIRCLE STAMPS

Circular sponges provide overall stamped texture, while brush wiping creates underlying interest.

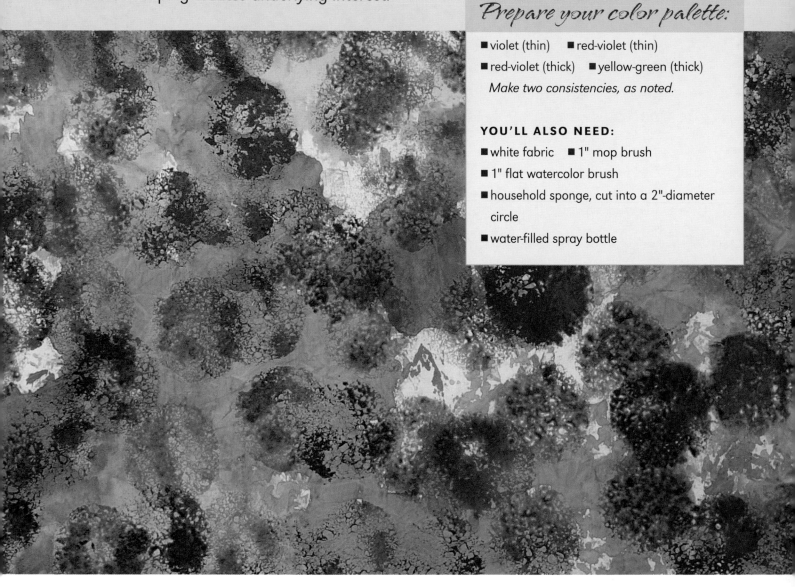

Prepare your color palette:

- violet (thin)   ■ red-violet (thin)
- red-violet (thick)   ■ yellow-green (thick)
  Make two consistencies, as noted.

YOU'LL ALSO NEED:
- white fabric   ■ 1" mop brush
- 1" flat watercolor brush
- household sponge, cut into a 2"-diameter circle
- water-filled spray bottle

1. Dampen the fabric. Dip a 1" mop brush in violet paint (or use a wet brush from another project). Use the fabric to wipe the brush. Repeat the wiping process with thin red-violet paint. Allow the fabric to dry thoroughly.

2. Lay the fabric flat. Dampen the sponge circle. Use a 1" flat watercolor brush to apply thick red-violet paint to it. Stamp the sponge onto the fabric surface at random, reloading with paint as desired. Rinse the brush and the sponge thoroughly when finished.

3. Repeat Step 2 using yellow-green paint. Lay the fabric flat to dry.

DESIGN TIP: THE AMOUNT OF PAINT ON THE SPONGE WILL DETERMINE HOW MUCH OF THE SPONGE'S ORIGINAL TEXTURE SHOWS THROUGH. MORE PAINT TRANSLATES TO LESS TEXTURE.

BRUSH STAMPING
AND BEYOND

Many different items can be used to stamp or print paint onto fabric. Look for objects that can hold the paint well and keep their own shape through repeated stampings. A paintbrush is a natural, once you get used to its stamping mode. Other ideas include wooden dowels, handprints, and leaves. Here are a few ideas to get you thinking.

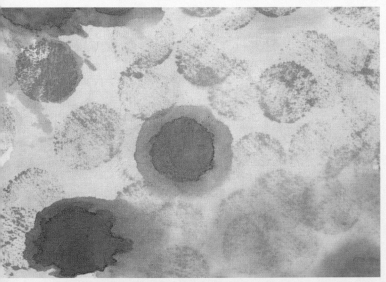

Dowel Stamping on Water-Splashed Fabric

■ **BRUSH STAMPING** Load the brush with paint and hold it horizontally to the fabric. Resist the urge to brush; instead, just press down gently to leave an impression. A large round house painting brush makes a rounded triangular shape. A flat brush makes a square or rectangle. A thin outlining brush makes a long, thin splat. The edge of a foam brush produces a rectangular form.

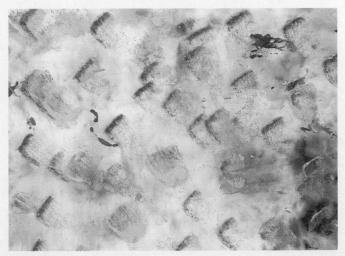

Brush Stamping

■ BLOTCHING A brush that is fully loaded will leave a blotch of paint where it first touches the fabric. This feature can be exploited. Touch down on very wet fabric and then drag the brush to create a large blotch surrounded by a halo.

Blotching

■ STIPPLING Stippling is a drawing technique that uses very small dots for shading. The effect can be mimicked with paint. Lightly dip a large round brush in paint, hold the brush vertically, and quickly stamp on the fabric in an up-and-down motion. The amount of fabric moisture determines whether the dots will diffuse.

Stippling

■ HAND STAMPING Paint the palm of your gloved hand with a paintbrush and then pat that hand on the fabric. A dry fabric will show creases in the glove more readily. Lightly spritzed fabric will diffuse the paint more.

Hand Stamping

■ LEAF PRINTING Flat, stiff leaves make excellent prints. Brush the paint onto the leaf surface, going out beyond the edges. Then place the leaf paint side down on lightly spritzed fabric and roll with a roller. I use a section of PVC pipe. The same technique can be used to print other flat shapes, such as cardboard cutouts.

Leaf Printing

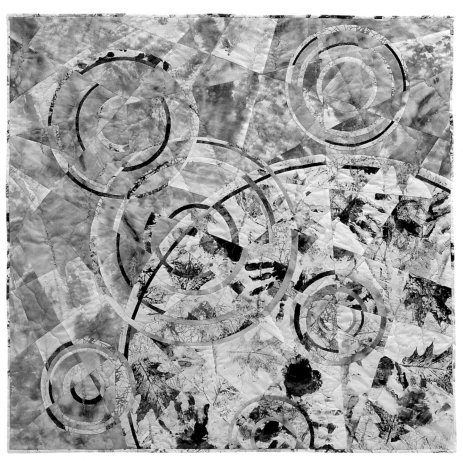

3 a.m. December 2002, Sue Beevers, 2003, 42$^1/_2$" x 42$^1/_2$". Hand- and machine-pieced, machine-embroidered, machine-quilted, beading.

DOUBLE EXPOSURE

The roller picks up wet paint residue during this printing process and transfers it to the fabric, for a shadow effect.

Prepare your color palette:

- red-violet
  Make a thick consistency.

YOU'LL ALSO NEED:

- yellow-orange fabric
- another piece of fabric (see Step 3)
- Pebeo Gold Glitter Finish
- bleach
- leaf
- 1" foam brush
- measuring cup
- plastic container
- white vinegar
- 1" flat watercolor brush
- 3" PVC pipe (for roller)
- measuring spoons
- plastic-wrapped board

1. Lay the yellow-orange fabric flat. Mix 1 cup water and 1 tablespoon bleach, for a discharge solution. Use a 1" flat watercolor brush to apply the solution onto the fabric in a striped pattern. Let sit for about 3 minutes, or just long enough for the dilute solution to remove some color without weakening the fibers. In the meantime, mix 1 pint water and 2 tablespoons vinegar. Place the fabric in this solution to stop the discharging reaction.

2. Wash, dry, and iron the discharged fabric. Lay it flat on the painting surface.

3. Place the leaf on the extra piece of fabric. Use a 1" flat watercolor brush to apply red-violet paint to the leaf. Start in the center and brush out and beyond the leaf edges to ensure complete coverage.

4. Place the leaf, paint side down, on the discharged fabric. Roll over the leaf with a PVC pipe section to transfer the paint. Carefully lift and remove the leaf.

5. Repeat Steps 3 and 4 to print more leaves on the discharged fabric. As you work, the roller will pick up some of the wet paint residue and transfer it back onto the fabric, creating "double exposure" shadow images. The extra piece of fabric, meanwhile, will show lots of reverse leaf designs and could become an interesting background fabric for a future painting session.

6. Lay the fabric flat and let it dry thoroughly. Use a 1" foam brush to apply a light coat of gold glitter finish.

TOOL TIP: THERE IS NO RIGHT OR WRONG SIDE WHEN YOU'RE PAINTING A LEAF TO PRINT. EACH SIDE WILL GIVE A SLIGHTLY DIFFERENT EFFECT, AND EACH LEAF IS DIFFERENT. EXPERIMENT TO DISCOVER WHICH SIDE OF THE LEAF LOOKS BETTER TO YOU.

FINGERPRINTS

Your own hand, gloved and painted, can become a
fabric stamping tool.

1. Wet the fabric thoroughly and lay it flat. Use a 1" flat
watercolor brush to randomly brush transparent yellow-
orange and green paint onto the wet fabric surface. To
encourage color blending, do not rinse the brush between
color changes. Let dry completely.

2. Lightly spritz the dry fabric with water. Put on latex
gloves. Brush opaque dark green paint onto the palm side
of one glove. Occasionally add dabs of white or yellow
paint to the glove, in addition to the green.

3. To make a hand print, press your gloved hand down
onto the damp fabric and then lift up. Repaint the glove
and repeat, rotating your hand and/or the fabric at random after each hand print. For some prints, use red-violet
opaque paint instead of green, rinsing the glove thoroughly
at color changes. Discard the glove when finished.

4. Lay the fabric flat to dry.

DESIGN TIP: A THIN COAT OF PAINT ON THE GLOVE
WILL HIGHLIGHT BOTH THE HAND AND THE GLOVE
CREASES IN THE PRINT.

STENCILING

A stencil is a flat card with one or more cutout openings that let you paint positive images on the fabric surface. A stencil can be used again and again, making it easy to cover a large area in a relatively short session. Making your own stencils helps you get exactly the look that you want.

■ **MAKING A STENCIL** Choose a flat nonporous material that is easy to cut with an X-Acto knife. Soft plastic lids with the rims cut off are just the right size for small stencils. Medium-weight stencil plastic and Mylar film, available at art supply stores, are also possibilities. My favorite stencils are cut from file folders and index cards. I coat both sides with acrylic paint so they're water-resistant.

To cut a stencil, place the card or plastic on a piece of heavy cardboard or pressboard. Cut out the motif with an X-Acto knife, using firm, even pressure. Cut away from yourself whenever possible, and try not to lift the blade from the surface. Change the blade as soon as it becomes dull to avoid slipping.

■ **STENCIL DESIGNS** I find that geometric shapes and small abstract curvilinear motifs work best for free-form stenciling. Start by drawing the motif on the stencil material. If the motif is to repeat within a geometric grid, draw the grid only, and then cut the motif freehand within the boundaries. It is not necessary to repeat the motif exactly or to cut out every space on the grid.

Incomplete Grids

Slight imperfections add visual interest to the stenciled motif. The sides of a square do not need to be perfectly straight. Motifs that repeat do not need to be exactly the same. Variations in size, shape, and alignment bring an element of surprise.

■ USING A STENCIL Position the stencil on the fabric and hold down the edges with your fingers. Very lightly dip the brush in the paint and wipe off the excess. Start at the outside edge of the cutout opening and work in toward the center, using a circular motion and very little pressure to apply the paint to the fabric. A light touch will prevent paint seepage and blotching.

If you have trouble with this dry brush technique, try spritzing the fabric very lightly. Paint will glide over the surface with minimal diffusion. To minimize smudging, use a thick opaque paint that dries quickly, such as PROfab. When transparent color is needed, I use a 1:1 mixture of Golden Fluid Acrylic paint and Silk Screen Fabric Gel.

■ SPECIAL EFFECTS Stencils can be placed anywhere on the fabric that you choose. They don't have to be oriented horizontally or vertically. They can be canted at various angles and even placed over themselves.

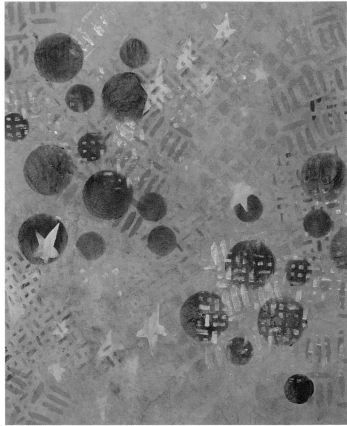

Overlapping Motifs

Randomly Placed Motifs

Identical Overlapping Motifs

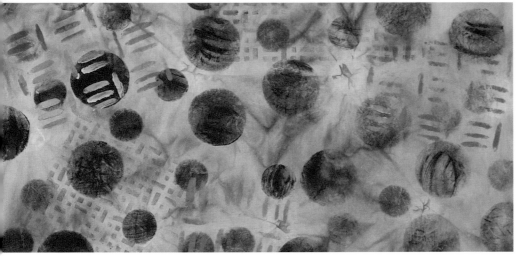

Combining Motifs

For clean, crisp edges, choose a densely woven fabric with a smooth surface. Freshly stenciled motifs can be spritzed with water if a softer look is desired. It is not necessary to paint the entire stencil or to use the same color throughout. The stencil can be flipped and painted from the reverse side. A wet, painted stencil can be lightly spritzed with water, flipped facedown on the fabric, and rubbed to make a reverse print on the fabric.

Using Multiple Colors

Reverse Prints

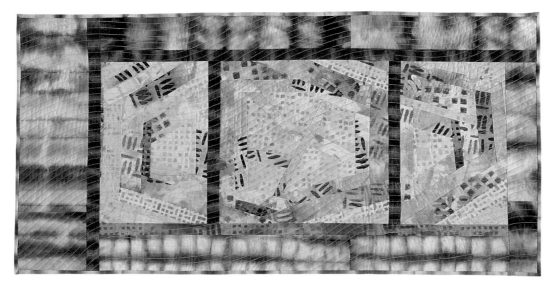

Sundogs,
Kathryn Stenstrom,
2003, 41" x 21".
Machine-pieced,
machine-quilted.

STENCILED **WRINKLES**

Stenciling over wrinkled fabric allows the stenciled image to be crisp in some places, less crisp in others. The result is easy but dramatic textural depth.

Prepare your color palette:

- violet (thin) ■ blue-violet (thick)
- red-violet (thick)

Make two consistencies, as noted.

YOU'LL ALSO NEED:
- 1 fat quarter (18" x 22" piece of fabric)
- stencil: $1/4$" x $1/4$" squares and $1/4$" x $1/2$" rectangles in a random grid
- stencil: $3/8$" x $3/8$" squares and $3/8$" x $3/4$" rectangles in a random grid
- 1" flat watercolor brush
- water-filled spray bottle
- measuring spoons
- zip-close plastic sandwich bag

1. Thoroughly dampen a fat quarter, bunch it up, and place it in a plastic bag. Do not compress the fabric. Use a measuring spoon to dribble 3 tablespoons thin violet paint over the fabric. Seal the bag. Let sit at least 20 minutes, or until the paint is absorbed. Remove the fabric from the bag and allow it to dry thoroughly.

2. Lay the fabric flat, without attempting to smooth the wrinkles. Place the smaller-motif stencil on top. Dip the leading edge of a 1" flat watercolor brush into thick blue-violet paint. Wipe off the excess on a spare cloth so that the brush is almost dry. With the bristles almost flat, very lightly brush across the stencil openings, just so the top-most wrinkles take some color.

3. Reposition the stencil in the same orientation to stencil the grid over the entire fabric surface. Add a few drops of red-violet to the blue-violet paint as the stenciling progresses. Rinse the brush thoroughly.

4. Repeat Steps 2 and 3 using the larger-motif stencil and the red-violet paint.

5. Lay the fabric flat to dry.

PAINTBOX TIP: USE THICK PAINT ON DRY FABRIC FOR A CLEAN, WELL-DEFINED STENCILED EDGE. TO SOFTEN THE EDGE WITHOUT SPRITZING, WIPE THE BRUSH CLEAN AND THEN STROKE THE DRY BRUSH OVER THE FABRIC.

POSITIVE-NEGATIVE

This yellow and white positive/negative effect is created by stenciling on a brush-wiped fabric.

Prepare your color palette:

- yellow (medium)　　■ yellow (thick)
- white (thick)

  Make two consistencies, as noted.

YOU'LL ALSO NEED:

- natural-colored fabric
- stencil: 1/4" x 1/4" squares and 1/4" x 1/2" rectangles in a random grid
- stencil: 3/8" x 3/8" squares and 3/8" x 3/4" rectangles in a random grid
- 1" flat watercolor brush
- 1 1/2" mop brush

1. Dip a 1 1/2" mop brush into medium yellow paint. Wipe the brush with the natural-colored fabric to transfer the color. Repeat as desired. Allow the fabric to dry thoroughly.

2. Iron the fabric to remove the wrinkles (see the Paint Comparison Chart on page 93 for details on when to iron).

3. Lay the fabric flat. Place the larger-motif stencil on an unpainted area of the fabric. Mix the yellow and white thick paints together in a 1:1 ratio. Dip a 1" flat watercolor brush into the paint. Wipe off the excess on a spare cloth so that the brush is almost dry. Brush across the stencil to paint the fabric. Reposition the stencil to a new unpainted area and repeat the process.

4. Place the smaller-motif stencil on a yellow area of the fabric. Load the watercolor brush with opaque white paint, but this time, do not shed the excess. Brush across the stencil. Move the stencil and repeat the process. The additional paint will cause splotching. These white splotches will relate directly to the yellow splotches created by brush wiping at the beginning.

5. Lay the fabric flat to dry.

DESIGN TIP: TO AVOID A STATIC VISUAL EFFECT, ORIENT THE STENCIL A LITTLE DIFFERENTLY EACH TIME.

MASKING

A mask works like a stencil in reverse. It prevents the paint from reaching the fabric surface, resulting in a negative image. Stencil materials and various tapes make good masks, as do flat, nonporous objects such as leaves. A leaf mask can be held down in the center with a finger. It doesn't need to be taped to the fabric.

Masking tape, clear packing tape, and Scotch tape let you paint perfectly straight lines. Don't use duct tape. It is very, very, very difficult to remove.

Con-Tact paper with its peel-off backing is my favorite masking material. The sticky underside ensures that all edges make firm contact with the surface, yet the masks can be lifted and repositioned on dry fabric many times. If the fabric is wet, use a hair dryer to spot-dry the sections you want to mask.

Leaf Mask

■ **STICKY MASKS** Masking materials with self-stick backings are very easy to work with. Freezer paper is good for very large masks. It is easy to cut and you can achieve thin, sharp points. To adhere the mask, place it shiny side down on dry fabric. Press with a warm iron, especially around the edges.

Tape Mask

■ PAINTING WITH MASKS

I use either a 1:1 mix of Golden Fluid Acrylic paint and Silk Screen Fabric Gel or PROfab opaque textile paint. The Golden mixture dries slowly. If the fabric around the mask is slightly dampened, a soft edge forms. The PROfab paint dries more quickly. To produce a heathered effect, use a lightly loaded dry brush and stroke gently.

Sponge-Stamped Mask

■ SPECIAL EFFECTS
Masks placed freely on the fabric surface add wonderful embellishment. Try turning the mask slightly each time it is moved. Remember that it is not necessary to paint around the entire edge of the mask or to stick to one color. The mask can be removed and repositioned as soon as it has been painted.

Different Mask Positions

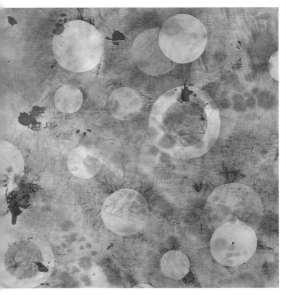

Dry Brush Heathering

Paint should be applied in a thin layer. If you are using a brush, a gentle circular motion works best. Brush from the center of the mask outward, never toward the mask, or paint will seep under the edge. For crisply defined motifs, especially when Con-Tact paper or tape masks are used, work on a dry, densely woven fabric with a smooth surface. Wet fabric does not work well. The paint sneaks under the edge of the mask as it diffuses.

Splattering or light stamping with a sponge is another way to paint over masks.

Stencils and masks can be used together. If a stencil cutout is large enough, it can become a mask. Using the stencil and its cutout together will create positive/negative images. Placing a mask under a stencil will make a negative shape within the stenciled motif.

Invisible City, Kathryn Stenstrom, 2003, 32" x 28". Machine-pieced, machine-quilted.

THE **PLANETS**

Masks, paint streaks, and a wrinkled surface
underneath combine to make this fabric.

Prepare your color palette:

- yellow (medium)   - yellow-orange (thick)
- green (thick)

Make two consistencies, as noted.

YOU'LL ALSO NEED:

- fabric
- clear Con-Tact paper
- 1" flat watercolor brush
- hair dryer
- scissors
- plastic containers

1. Fill a small plastic container partway with water, add a few drops of yellow paint, and stir. Dip the fabric into the water and remove immediately. Wring out the excess moisture. Allow to dry thoroughly.

2. Cover the painting surface with a wrinkled plastic bag. Lay the fabric flat on top.

3. Use scissors to cut several circles and rings, 3/4" to 2" in diameter, from Con-Tact paper. Remove the paper backings and adhere the masks to the fabric. Strive for a random design; avoid placing the masks in a straight line or grid.

4. Touch a 1" flat watercolor brush to thick yellow-orange paint, just enough to color the bristles. Lightly stroke the brush across the masked area of the fabric. A dark streak will occur where the brush first touches down. As the paint

on the brush diminishes, start at the center of the mask and work outward, brushing around the mask in a circular motion. Repeat the entire process with thick green paint. It isn't necessary to rinse the brush prior to color changes.

5. Remove and reposition some of the masks. Use a hair dryer to spot-dry the new locations if necessary—the masks will not stick to damp fabric. Repeat the Step 4 painting process. Continue in this manner, changing some of the masks and keeping others in place, to develop the design.

6. Lay the fabric flat to dry.

TOOL TIP: USE CLEAR CON-TACT PAPER FOR MASKS. YOU WILL BE ABLE TO SEE WHAT IS UNDERNEATH EACH MASK, EVEN THOSE THAT ARE STACKED.

FREE-FORM **PLAID**

A plaid pattern is easy to create with tape masks. Thin vertical and horizontal lines, painted freehand, add to the illusion.

Prepare your color palette:

- red-violet (medium)
- red-violet (thick)
- yellow-green (thick)
- dark green (thick)

Make two consistencies, as noted.

YOU'LL ALSO NEED:

- fabric
- masking tape
- plastic bag
- plastic container
- 2" clear packing tape
- 1" flat watercolor brush
- #3 outliner brush

1. Fill a small plastic container partway with water, add a few drops of medium red-violet paint, and stir. Dip the fabric into the water and remove immediately. Wring out the excess moisture. Allow to dry thoroughly.

2. Cover the painting surface with a wrinkled plastic bag. Lay the fabric flat on top.

3. Run a length of masking tape horizontally across the fabric surface. Press to adhere. Dip a 1" flat watercolor brush into thick red-violet paint, just enough to load the tips of the bristles. Lightly stroke the brush in a circular motion along each edge of the mask. Do not remove the tape.

4. Run a length of 2" packing tape vertically on the fabric surface. Press to adhere. Once again, use a circular motion to lightly brush thick red-violet paint along each edge of the mask. Do not remove the tape.

5. Repeat Steps 3 and 4, positioning horizontal and vertical masks on the fabric and stroking along the edges to develop the design. Vary the tape placement, tape width, and color choices to avoid exact repetition. Every once in a while, load a #3 outliner brush with dark green or yellow-green paint and paint a thin line parallel to the newest tape.

6. Lay the fabric flat to dry.

DIPPING TIP: TO CREATE AN IRREGULAR BACK-GROUND TINT, CHOOSE A RELATIVELY SMALL CONTAINER FOR DIPPING. WHEN THE FABRIC IS BUNCHED UP INSIDE THE CONTAINER, THE PAINT WILL REACH SOME AREAS BUT NOT OTHERS.

MONOPRINTING

Monoprinting is a technique for making a single print from a freshly painted surface. It's easily adaptable to fabric painting. You'll need paint, brushes, a printing plate, and a roller. A piece of Plexiglas slightly smaller than the fabric makes a good printing plate. A 3"-diameter PVC pipe works well as a roller. Have it cut slightly longer than the printing plate.

■ **PAINTING THE PLATE** The first step is to paint the printing plate. Pebeo and PROfab paints are suitable, but they dry fast, so you will need to work fairly quickly. Spritzing the painted plate very lightly with water helps keep things moist. Golden paint mixed with Print Base Medium has a longer open time. It isn't necessary to paint the entire plate. Unpainted areas add interest to the fabric.

■ **PULLING THE PRINT** Carefully place the fabric over the painted surface. Either dry or lightly spritzed fabric can be used. I don't recommend wet fabric. The paint diffuses too much, obliterating the design on the printing plate. For a smooth, uninterrupted color flow, iron the fabric first. For random disruptions in the pattern, crumple the fabric before you lay it down.

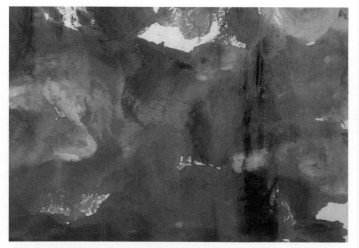

Unpainted Areas

Printed Wrinkles

Gently pat the fabric (wear latex gloves), starting at the center and moving outwards. Your goal is to remove air bubbles and wrinkles. Next, roll the fabric with your PVC pipe section to ensure that paint reaches the entire fabric surface. Just one pass is sufficient. Subsequent rolling will spread and blend the paint too much, and the monoprint effect will be lost.

■ SPECIAL EFFECTS Paint consistency is the factor that most controls the outcome of this technique. Thick paint covers the plate completely and is easy to apply. The brush strokes will show where the paint layer is thinner.

Visible Brush Strokes

Another interesting approach is to splatter thick paint over a layer of thin paint. When the fabric is rolled, the splatters flatten out.

Monoprint Splatters

Bubbly Texture

Medium to thin paint forms tiny beads on the plate. This is true of every paint brand. The thinner the paint or the application, the more the beads will form. Monoprinting is the only way to achieve this bubbly texture. It is most pronounced if a dry, densely woven fabric is used. Lightly spritzed or damp fabric will allow the beads to diffuse and blend.

A more spontaneous form of monoprinting uses the paint residue from a previously painted fabric. Lightly spritz the painting surface with water. Wait a few minutes for beads to form, or spread the paint residue around the surface with a brush, and then make a print. If the painting surface was initially covered with a wrinkled plastic bag, your print will pick up that texture too.

Textured Paint Residue

About My Life, Sue Beevers, 2003, 41½" x 42½". Machine-pieced, paper-pieced, hand-appliquéd, machine-quilted.

FALLING **LEAVES**

Stenciling and leaves combine in this monoprinted fabric.

1. Lay the fabric flat. Spritz lightly with water.

2. Use a 2" foam brush and medium-consistency yellow-green, blue, and yellow-orange paint to paint rectangles and squares of various sizes on the Plexiglas plate. Rinse the brush between color changes.

3. Lay the fabric on the painted plate. Starting at one edge, roll a PVC pipe over the fabric to transfer the paint. One pass is sufficient; the more you roll, the more the paint will blend, obliterating the effect. Carefully lift the fabric off the plate. Lay the fabric flat to dry.

4. Place a stencil on the fabric. Touch a 1" flat watercolor brush into yellow-green, yellow, or white opaque paint, loading 2 or more colors at a time. Starting in the middle of the stencil, rub the paint in a circular motion onto the fabric through the stencil cutouts. It is not necessary to use the same color throughout the entire stencil or to paint all of the stencil spaces. Reposition the stencil and repeat as desired. Lay the fabric flat to dry.

5. Use a 1" flat watercolor brush to apply thick dark green paint or Pebeo Copper Shimmer paint to a leaf. Place the leaf, paint side down, on the fabric and roll with a PVC pipe roller to make a print. Repeat as desired. Let the fabric dry.

6. Use a 1" foam brush to apply streaks of Pebeo Gold Glitter Finish to the fabric. Lay the fabric flat to dry.

PAINTBOX TIP: PAINT THE PRINTING PLATE VERY QUICKLY, SO THAT THE PAINT DOESN'T DRY OUT BEFORE YOU CAN PRINT IT. VERY LIGHTLY SPRITZ THE PAINTED PLATE IF YOU NOTICE THAT IT IS DRYING TOO QUICKLY.

DOUBLEHEADER

With care and a certain amount of speed, two fabrics can be printed from the same monoprinting plate. Here, the left fabric was printed first. Then the plate was spritzed with water and reused to print the fabric at the right.

First Printing

Second Printing

Prepare your color palette:

- red - yellow - blue - green

Make all a thick consistency.

YOU'LL ALSO NEED:

- 2 pieces of fabric
- Plexiglas printing plate
- 1" foam brush
- water-filled spray bottle
- 3" PVC pipe (for roller)

1. Thoroughly spritz one piece of fabric with water and set it aside.

2. Use a 1" foam brush to paint red, yellow, blue, and green square outlines on the Plexiglas plate. Make each outline a different size. Rinse the brush between color changes. Work quickly to paint a new, different colored square outline within each painted square. Continue painting smaller squares within the squares, varying the colors. Spritz the plate lightly with water as needed to keep the paint moist.

3. Lay the dry fabric on the plate and roll with a PVC pipe to transfer the paint. Carefully lift the fabric off the plate. Lay the fabric flat to dry.

4. Immediately spritz the plate lightly with water. Place the damp fabric from Step 1 on the plate and make a second print. Lift the fabric and lay it flat to dry.

FABRIC TIP: WET FABRIC ENCOURAGES PAINT TO DIFFUSE AND MIGRATE. IT IS PERFECT FOR PRINTING FROM A PREVIOUSLY PRINTED PLATE.

RESIST
TECHNIQUES

VEGETAL STARCH RESIST

A vegetal starch resist is a pastelike substance that is applied to fabric to prevent paint from adhering. It results in a characteristic overall crackled texture. The idea of using common foodstuffs—wheat flour, cornstarch, oatmeal, rice—as paint resist continues to fascinate me. The resist recipes and techniques presented here are a result of many, many hours of experimentation.

Brush-Stamped Resist

Flour resist can be used in an uncooked form or as a cooked paste. Cornstarch, oatmeal, and rice resists are always cooked. Each resist has unique properties. Uncooked flour paste is very delicate. The crackle lines form easily, and the fabric must be handled carefully to avoid chipping. Cornstarch and rice paste resist have the smoothest texture and are good for fine lines and details. All cooked paste resists work well in large surface applications, where they can be applied with a sponge or paintbrush. They don't break down quickly when wet and will not crackle easily. To encourage crackling, let the resist dry. Then crumple the fabric, hold two diagonally opposite corners, and give the fabric a quick snap.

Blue Poles Too, Colleen Mullen Bolton, 2003, Diptych Part A: 13^1/$_8$" x 21^1/$_4$"; Part B: 20^3/$_8$" x 21^1/$_4$". Machine-pieced, hand-quilted.

■ UNCOOKED FLOUR RESIST

This resist is a 1:1 mixture of flour and cold water. Carefully sprinkle the flour into the water, stirring continuously. Allow the mixture to sit for a few minutes, then stir again to remove any residual small lumps. The resist is now ready to use.

To apply the resist, pour a small amount onto dry fabric. Spread it with a 4" spackling knife, available at any hardware store, until the surface is very smooth. A thin layer will allow for a lot of fine crackle lines.

A thicker layer will form thicker lines.

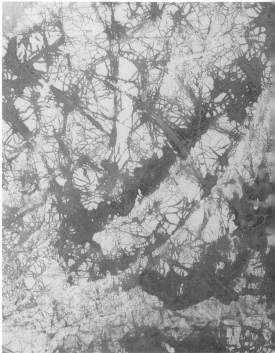

Thick Application

Use a trowel or knife with a slotted edge, such as a linoleum adhesive applicator, to make textured swirls and geometric designs.

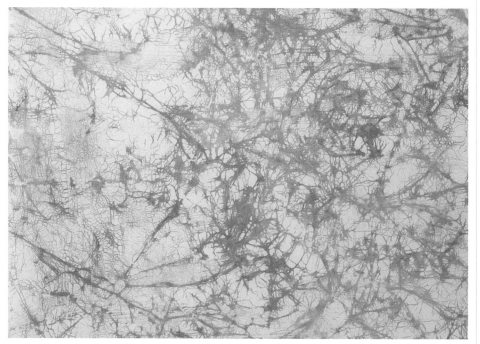

Thin Application

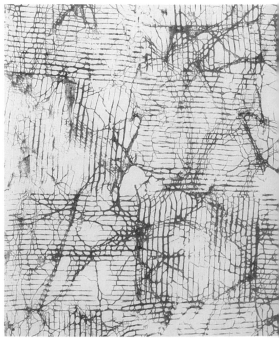

Slotted Edge Design

■ **COOKED FLOUR PASTE** This is my favorite flour paste recipe. Its thick grain makes it suitable for everything except fine details. Thoroughly mix $1/4$ cup flour and 1 cup cold water and boil for 1 minute. Cool only slightly; this resist is easier to apply while warm and, like all cooked resists, will thicken as it cools. Try dribbling the warm resist from a spoon. Thinning the cooled resist with water makes it easier to apply, but a halo will form around the resisted area.

Warm Dribbled Resist

■ **COOKED CORNSTARCH PASTE** Mix 2 tablespoons cornstarch and 1 cup cold water and boil for 1 minute. This smooth, fine-grained resist is particularly nice to use in a squeeze bottle to make fine lines. It must be used while still warm; cooled cornstarch paste is jellylike and difficult to apply.

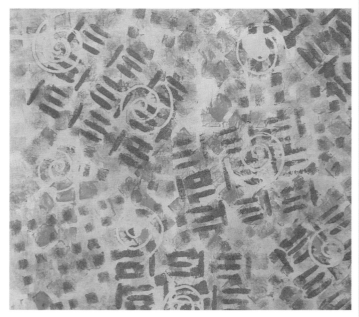

Squeeze Bottle Swirls

■ **COOKED RICE PASTE** I use two different methods to make rice paste. Once made, both pastes work exactly the same.

Method 1: Stir 3 tablespoons rice flour into 1 cup cold water. Bring the mixture to a full boil for 1 minute. Remove from heat. Stir in 1 tablespoon cold water.

Method 2: Add 1 cup white rice to $3^1/2$ cups cold water. Cook on medium heat for 20 minutes. Drain the rice, saving the water. Boil the rice water on medium heat for an additional 15 minutes. Stir every few minutes. It will reach the consistency of heavy syrup.

Rice paste has the finest grain of all the vegetal starch resists. Because it has very good resisting properties, it works well for stenciling and leaf printing. It can be used at any temperature. It is thinner when it is warm, and it can be easily applied with a brush when it cools.

Rice Paste Resist with Oak Leaves

■ *Dump the Lumps. Cooked cornstarch, rice, and flour paste resist must be lump-free. Cook them over a low heat, stirring constantly with a wire whisk to prevent lumps and to avoid burning. Once cooked, pour the hot paste through a mesh strainer. The paste can be used as soon as it cools a bit.*

■ COOKED OATMEAL PASTE Use rolled oats (the old-fashioned kind) to make oatmeal paste resist. Processed "quick" oats and instant oatmeals will not work as well. Combine 1 cup water and $\frac{1}{3}$ cup rolled oats. Allow the mixture to boil for 3 minutes. Oatmeal paste can be applied warm or cool. It is best when applied over large areas. Crumple and snap the fabric to encourage crackling.

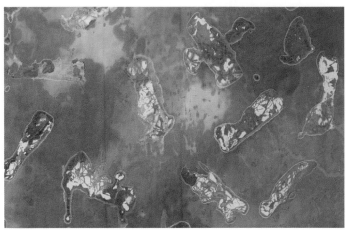

Breaching a Thin Resist

Oatmeal Resist Texture

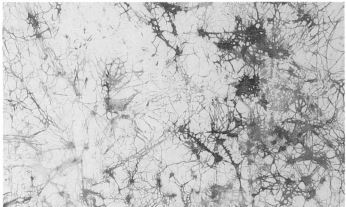

Large Resisted Area

■ WORKING WITH PASTE RESIST Be careful not to apply any resist too thickly: it will take forever to dry. A thin application is all that is needed. The resisted fabric must be laid flat to dry. When the resist is completely dry, the fabric is ready to paint.

Once you start applying the paint, you must work fast, finishing before the resist succumbs to the added moisture. Uncooked flour resist in particular breaks down very quickly when exposed to wet paint. Use a medium to thick paint consistency; thin paint will breach the resist sooner. Breaching can also occur if the resist did not penetrate to the underside of the fabric.

Apply paint to the resisted side of the fabric. Be aware that the paint will cover the resist as well as the fabric. The fabric will look very different once the resist is removed. The paint will show only in unresisted areas and where the resist has cracked or been breached.

■ REMOVING PASTE RESIST When the painting is complete, the fabric must once again be laid flat to dry. Never heat-set a resisted fabric. Heating causes the resist to cook and imbed into the fabric, making it nearly impossible to remove. Instead, follow the passive color setting time recommended by the paint manufacturer (see the Paint Comparison Chart on page 93).

Once the color has set, the resist can be removed and the fabric laundered. Soak the fabric in clear, warm water for 15 to 20 minutes. Multiple fabric pieces can be stacked in the water. Flour and oatmeal resist can be removed by light scrubbing with a nail brush. Cornstarch and rice pastes are easily removed by gentle rubbing. It is very important that all of the resist is removed. Insects and mice just love to munch on vegetal starch. Once the resist is removed, the fabric can be hand-laundered as usual.

SWIRLY **STRIPES**

Create this pattern by applying uncooked flour resist with a notched trowel.

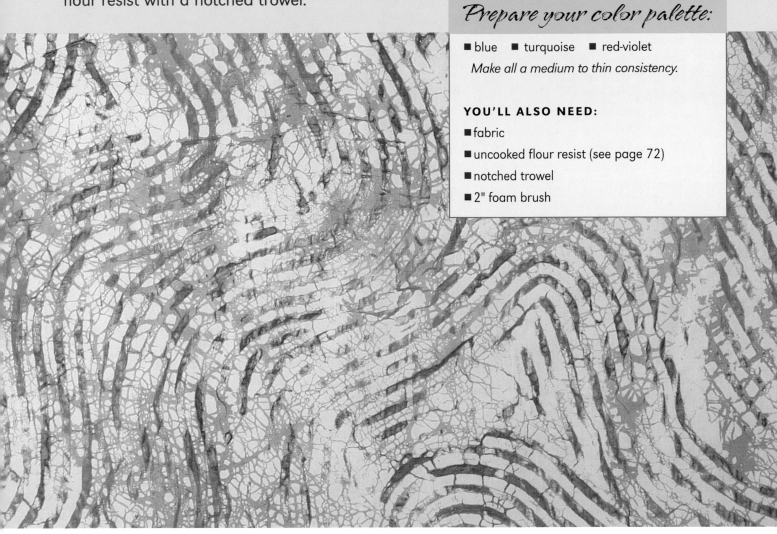

Prepare your color palette:

- blue   - turquoise   - red-violet

Make all a medium to thin consistency.

YOU'LL ALSO NEED:

- fabric
- uncooked flour resist (see page 72)
- notched trowel
- 2" foam brush

1. Lay the fabric flat. Pour some flour resist onto the fabric and spread it around with a notched trowel. Move the trowel in gentle swirls to create free-flowing concentric curves. Let the fabric dry thoroughly.

2. Gently crush the dry fabric into a loose wad to promote crackling in the resist. Be careful though—uncooked resist is very delicate and overhandling may cause small chunks to flake off. Open the fabric and lay it flat, resist side up.

3. Use a 2" foam brush to apply blue, then turquoise, and finally red-violet paint over the dried resist. Do not rinse the brush between color changes.

4. Lay the fabric flat. Let it rest, undisturbed, for 10 days, or until the paint is passively set. Remove the resist. Wash the fabric thoroughly by hand to remove any lingering particles.

TOOL TIP: TILE SETTERS USE A NOTCHED TROWEL TO APPLY MASTIC TO LARGE FLOOR TILES. YOU CAN USE MASTIC TO CREATE PERFECT CURVED STRIPES. FIND THIS TOOL AT HARDWARE STORES AND HOME IMPROVEMENT CENTERS.

IRRESISTIBLE

A rice paste resist is applied over a rich base fabric
that features paint colors left over from other projects.

Prepare your color palette:

- yellow-green ▪ yellow ▪ yellow-orange
*Use transparent paints. Make all a
medium consistency.*

YOU'LL ALSO NEED:
- base fabric (see Step 1)
- rice paste resist (see page 73)
- stencil: 3/4" x 3/4" squares in a random grid
- 1" flat watercolor brush
- 2" foam brush, notched

1. Choose a base fabric; the sample fabric was colored
by surface and brush wiping. Iron the fabric to remove any
wrinkles.

2. Lay the fabric flat. Place the stencil on top. Use a 1"
flat watercolor brush to apply the rice paste over the stencil
cutouts in a circular motion. Reposition the stencil, varying
the orientation, and repeat the application as desired.
Remember that it is not necessary to fill every space of the
stencil. Let the paste dry thoroughly.

3. Dip the 2" notched foam brush into 2 of the 3 transparent paint colors: yellow-green, yellow, and yellow-orange.
Brush the paint across the resist-treated surface.

Repeat with different color combinations, rinsing out the
brush when changing colors.

4. Lay the fabric flat. Let it rest, undisturbed, for 14 days,
or until the paint is passively set. Remove the resist and
wash the fabric thoroughly by hand. Let dry.

⊞ RESIST TIP: RICE PASTE IS A THIN RESIST THAT
SPREADS VERY EASILY. BE CAREFUL NOT TO USE A LOT OF
BRUSH PRESSURE OR APPLY TOO THICK A COATING. IF YOU
DO, THE PASTE WILL CRAWL BENEATH THE STENCIL AND
TRANSFER TO THE FABRIC AS A BLOTCH.

WATER-BASED GUTTA

Water-based gutta is a very stable resist that requires no preparation. Use it right out of the bottle, as is. Unlike vegetal starch resist, it will not crack.

■ **USING A STRETCHER FRAME** Gutta is applied to dry fabric that is held taut on a wooden stretcher frame. A frame (available at art supply stores) is important for several reasons. It makes the clear gutta easier to see. It also prevents splotches. Without a frame, gutta would seep through to the painting surface underneath, spread out, and be reabsorbed by the fabric.

Begin by stretching the fabric over the frame. Use pushpins to secure the fabric at the middle of the top and bottom edges. Then stretch and pin the middle of the side edges. Continue pinning out to each corner until the fabric is stretched taut but not tight.

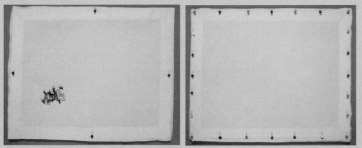

Pin at the middle of edges.   Work out toward the corners.

Leiwen, Sue Beevers, 2003, 33" x 43½". Wholecloth quilt, machine-quilted.

■ APPLYING THE GUTTA

Gutta resist can be applied by brushing or stamping. It can also be placed in a metal tip applicator bottle and used to draw fine lines on all or part of the fabric.

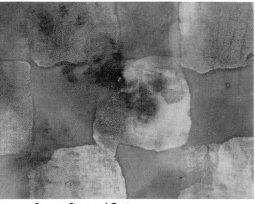

Sponge-Stamped Gutta

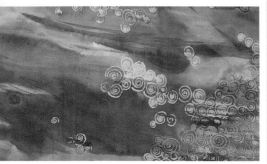

Spiral Lines

Because gutta is clear, areas or lines where the resist is applied will appear as the fabric's original color. You can tint those areas by adding a few drops of paint to the gutta the night before you use it. The pigment will stay behind when the gutta is rinsed out.

As with any liquid resist, care must be taken to ensure that the gutta penetrates to the underside of the fabric. To ensure a solid barrier, especially if a densely woven fabric is used, just flip the fabric over, frame and all, and retrace the design on the underside. Allow the gutta to dry thoroughly prior to painting.

■ PAINTING THE FABRIC

A gutta-resisted fabric can be painted using any paint and any technique. Just be careful not to use too much moisture, which can dissolve the gutta and lead to a barrier breach. A breach that is deliberate (or accidental) can be enhanced by spritzing freshly painted sections.

Breached Barrier

Remember that it isn't necessary to paint the entire fabric surface.

Partially Painted Surface

A particularly interesting effect is called walling-in. Just touch a loaded paintbrush to an area that is outlined in gutta. The paint will spread and diffuse until it reaches the gutta wall. Use medium to thin paint, and be careful not to overload the brush. You can also apply several colors within a single walled-in shape.

Walling-In

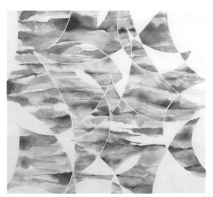

Multicolored Walling-In

■ REMOVING THE GUTTA

Avoid heat-setting the fabric, which will make the gutta very difficult to remove. Instead, follow the passive color setting time recommended by the paint manufacturer (see the Paint Comparison Chart on page 93). Hand-launder the fabric as usual. I find it helpful to soak the fabric in warm water for 10 to 15 minutes prior to washing to ensure that all of the gutta is easily removed.

CHRYSANTHEMUM **PETALS**

Water-soluble gutta resist was applied through a fine metal tip to outline these repeating flower petal motifs.

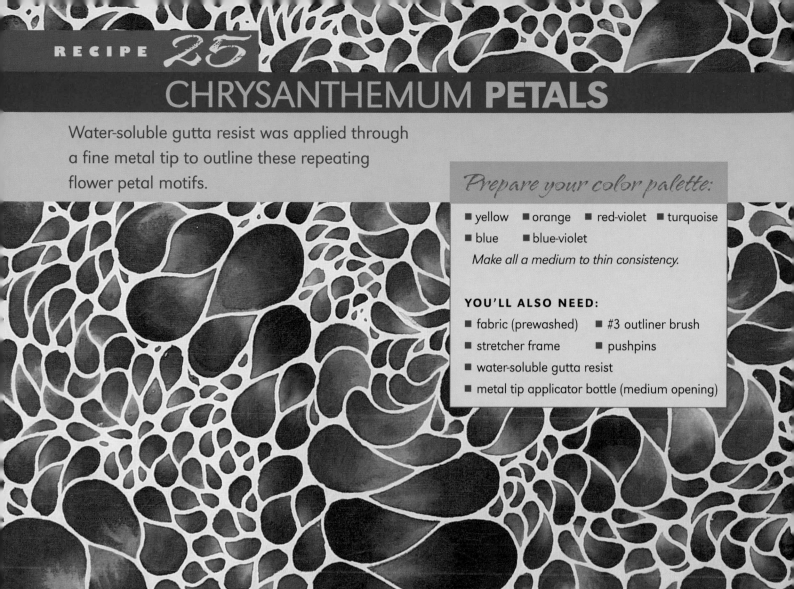

Prepare your color palette:

- yellow
- orange
- red-violet
- turquoise
- blue
- blue-violet

Make all a medium to thin consistency.

YOU'LL ALSO NEED:

- fabric (prewashed)
- #3 outliner brush
- stretcher frame
- pushpins
- water-soluble gutta resist
- metal tip applicator bottle (medium opening)

1. Secure the fabric in a stretcher frame, using pushpins to hold it taut. (See page 77.)

2. Use a metal tip applicator bottle to draw gutta resist lines on the fabric surface. Be sure to press the tip into the fabric slightly to ensure that the resist line is continuous. Without some pressure, the resist comes out in tiny beads and it will not form a solid barrier against the paint. The featured design has swirling petal shapes in various sizes. It is not necessary to draw the motif on the fabric beforehand; instead, let your inhibitions go and allow the design to develop freely. Do a small section at a time and then turn the frame over and retrace the lines on the reverse side. Continue in this way until the design is complete. Let the gutta resist dry overnight.

3. Select an area of the design to be painted in warm colors. Use a #3 outliner brush to paint each motif defined by the gutta resist barrier. Touch the loaded brush to the fabric, applying yellow paint at the pointed end of the motif, orange in the middle, and red-violet at the rounded

end, so that the colors blend into one another. Rinse the brush between color changes. Paint a small grouping of petals; then step back and take a look at your work.

4. Repeat Step 3 in a different area with cool colors. Use turquoise at the point, blue in the middle, and blue-violet at the rounded end of each petal motif.

5. Repeat Steps 3 and 4, painting small groups of petals with either warm or cool colors, until the entire design is filled.

6. Lay the fabric flat. Let it rest, undisturbed, until the paint is passively set (follow the manufacturer's recommendations). Soak the fabric in warm water for about 15 minutes to remove the gutta. Wash thoroughly by hand.

RESIST TIP: RESIST TAKES TIME TO DRY. TO AVOID SMUDGING EXISTING LINES OF RESIST AS YOU ARE APPLYING NEW ONES, START IN THE MIDDLE OF THE FABRIC AND WORK OUT. ROTATE THE FRAME AS YOU CONTINUE THE APPLICATION.

CROSSHATCH

Gutta resist not only acts as a paint barrier in this fabric, but also becomes a design element.

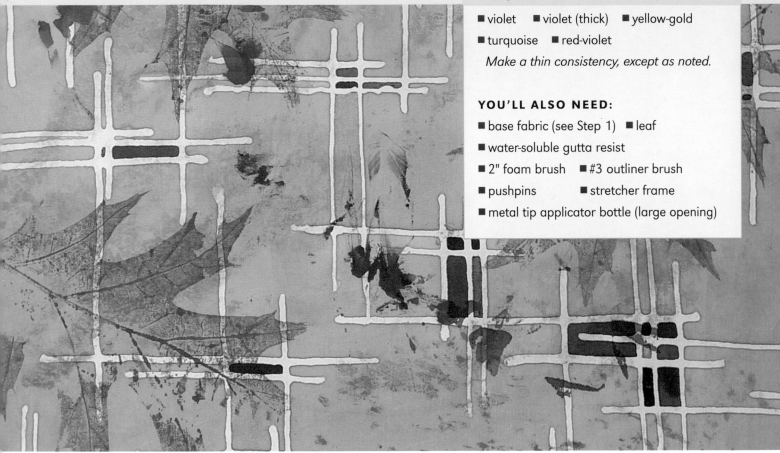

Prepare your color palette:

- violet   - violet (thick)   - yellow-gold
- turquoise   - red-violet

Make a thin consistency, except as noted.

YOU'LL ALSO NEED:
- base fabric (see Step 1)   - leaf
- water-soluble gutta resist
- 2" foam brush   - #3 outliner brush
- pushpins   - stretcher frame
- metal tip applicator bottle (large opening)

1. Choose a base fabric. The sample fabric was colored by wiping a painting surface with an ice cream stick.

2. Use a 2" foam brush to apply thick violet paint to a leaf. Print the leaf on the base fabric. Repeat as desired. Rinse out the brush. Allow the fabric to dry thoroughly.

3. Secure the fabric in a stretcher frame with pushpins to hold it taut. Use a metal tip applicator bottle to draw gutta cross-hatching on the fabric surface. Keep the cross-hatching on a vertical/horizontal axis but vary the overall placement. As you complete a section, turn the frame over and retrace the lines on the reverse side. Continue in this way until the design is complete. Let the gutta resist dry overnight.

4. Use a 2" foam brush to apply yellow-gold paint to the fabric. Leave some walled-in spaces unpainted. Use a #3 outliner brush to paint the remaining spaces turquoise, red-violet, or violet. Rinse the brush between color changes.

5. Lay the fabric flat. Let it rest, undisturbed, to passively set the colors (follow the manufacturer's recommendations). Soak the fabric in warm water for about 15 minutes to remove the gutta resist. Wash by hand.

DESIGN TIP: EVERY FEW MINUTES, TAKE A STEP BACK AND EVALUATE YOUR RESIST LINES. DON'T DRAW TOO MANY, OR THE FABRIC WILL HAVE A CROWDED LOOK. ALSO BE AWARE OF THE RELATIONSHIP BETWEEN LINE MOTIFS AND THE LEAF PATTERNS.

TWISTED AND FOLDED RESIST

 wisting and folding resist techniques rely on the fact that paint is unable to thoroughly penetrate layers of tightly compressed fabric. Fabric density and moisture, paint consistency, and the way the fabric is compressed work together to create these visual effects.

■ **TWISTED RESIST** Fabrics painted in this manner have a diagonal design.

Twisted Resist

Twist the fabric and wrap it around a juice can.

Hold a wet fat quarter at diagonally opposite corners. Twist the corners in opposite directions to make a tight roll. Use a rubber band to secure one end of the fabric twist to the top of a plastic juice can. Wrap the twisted roll around the can, and secure the loose end to the bottom of the can. An 11.5-ounce can will hold 2 fat quarters, or 1/2 yard of fabric.

Paint vertical, horizontal, or diagonal stripes on the fabric in different colors. Rotate the fabric roll a bit to be sure that the side touching the can gets painted.

Paint a striped pattern.

For crisp painted edges, allow the fabric to dry on the can before you remove it. Remember that dry, tightly twisted fabric will not allow the paint to penetrate the folds as readily as wet, loosely twisted fabric. Once the painted fabric is dry, it can be opened up, redampened, and retwisted, and the painting process repeated.

■ **FANFOLDING** Fanfolding is a simple process. Place the fabric on a flat surface and fold in one edge. Then flip the fabric over and make another fold. It is not necessary to crease the folds; hand patting along the fold line is sufficient.

Diagonal fanfolds are made by folding first one half of the fabric and then the other. The initial fold doesn't have to be from corner to corner, and the fabric doesn't have to be square. Don't bother to flip the fabric—the length of the fold will automatically decrease with each fold, and it will be difficult to keep the folds together. Flip the fabric only after completely folding the first half.

Diagonal Fanfolding

Fanfolded Fabric

The size of the fold determines the width of the finished stripe. If the folds are even, the stripes will be evenly spaced and parallel to each other. Unevenly folded fabric will be less formal.

Here are some variations to try:

Chevron. Fold the fabric in half, then make diagonal fanfolds.

Stripes. Fanfold the fabric, then roll up the strip.

Triangles. Fold the fabric in half; then make triangular fanfolds.

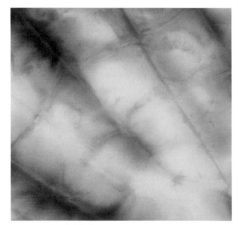

Uneven Fanfolded Stripes

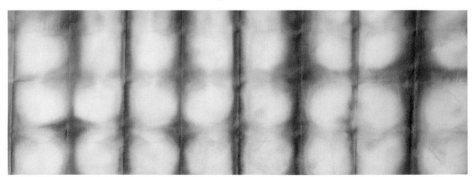

Plaid. Fanfold the fabric; then fanfold the folded strip.

Secure your folded or rolled fabric bundle with a rubber band around the middle. The rubber band should be tight enough to make the edges flare a bit.

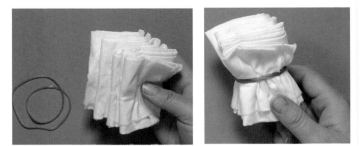

Folding and Securing a Fabric Bundle

■ PAINTING A FOLDED BUNDLE Begin by soaking the fabric bundle in water for a few minutes, or until it is thoroughly wet. Remove it from the water and squeeze out the excess moisture. It is now ready for painting.

The easiest way to paint the damp fabric bundle is to dip it, folded edge down, in about $1/4$" of paint and allow it to sit for a few minutes. Wicking action will pull the paint into the fabric. The bundle can then be flipped over and placed in the same or a different color. If the fabric bundle has been folded a second time, the unfolded edges can also be painted in the same manner. Be sure to let the fabric sit long enough to allow the inner folds to absorb some paint.

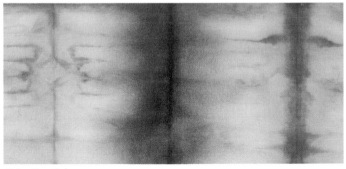

Using Two Colors

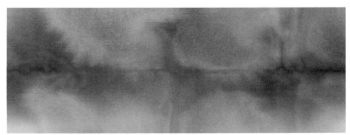

Wet Fanfolded Bundle, Rubber Band Removed

Removing the fabric bundle's rubber band prior to painting will allow the paint to migrate more readily. Migration will be more pronounced when the fabric is very wet.

After painting, remove the rubber band and unfold the fabric. Laying the fabric flat to dry will preserve the painted effect. Hanging the fabric will encourage the wet paint to diffuse and migrate downward, an effect you can encourage with light spritzing. Don't forget that the orientation of the hung fabric (stripes vertical or stripes horizontal) will affect the outcome. Watch the fabric carefully. Once you like the way it looks, lay it flat to complete drying.

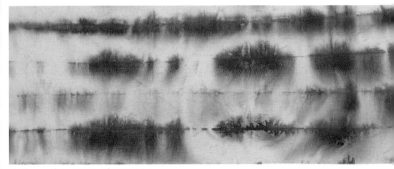

Diffusion from Vertical Hanging

Pinwheels and Petticoats, Gail Strout, 2002, $31^1/2$" x 39". Machine-pieced, machine-quilted, hand-appliquéd and fused.

BUNDLE **DIPPING**

This fabric was folded and painted three separate times.

Prepare your color palette:

■ yellow-green ■ blue ■ violet ■ red-violet
Make all a thin consistency.

YOU'LL ALSO NEED:
■ fabric ■ rubber band ■ ice cube tray

1. Lay the fabric flat. Fan-fold the fabric, roll it up, and secure it with a rubber band. Soak the fabric roll in a container of water for a few minutes, until thoroughly wet.

2. Put each paint color in its own ice cube tray compartment. Remove the roll from the water and squeeze gently to remove excess moisture. Dip one edge into yellow-green paint and let it sit for 30 seconds. Then dip the opposite edge into blue paint. Remove. Let the roll sit, blue edge up, for about 5 minutes, to allow the paint to migrate downward. Remove the rubber band, unfold the fabric, and lay it flat to dry.

3. Fan-fold the fabric again, but from a different direction. Instead of rolling the strip, make accordion folds, for a rectangular bundle. Secure with a rubber band. Soak the bundle in water until thoroughly damp.

4. Remove the bundle from the water and squeeze gently. Dip one edge into red-violet paint and then immediately redip in violet paint. Repeat for each edge. Remove the rubber band, unfold the fabric, and lay it flat to dry.

5. Repeat the Step 3 folding sequence once more. Add water to the red-violet paint and dip both ends of the bundle into this very dilute color. Undo the bundle and lay the fabric flat to dry.

PAINTBOX TIP: DIPPING AND REDIPPING CAN CREATE A MARVELOUS FABRIC. BE SURE THAT THE PAINT IS COMPLETELY DRY BETWEEN DIPPINGS, ESPECIALLY IF YOU USE COMPLEMENTARY COLORS, TO AVOID MUDDY BLENDS.

MORE BUNDLE DIPPING

Splatters add a wonderful finishing touch
to this bundled and dipped fabric.

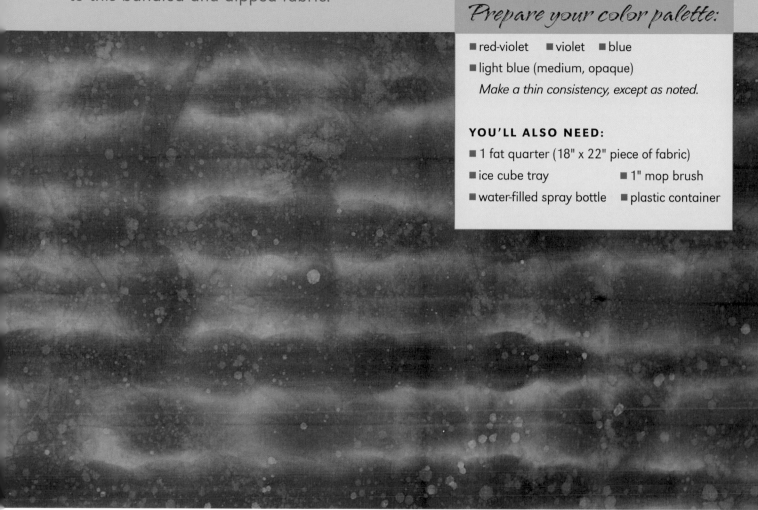

Prepare your color palette:

- red-violet   ■ violet   ■ blue
- light blue (medium, opaque)

Make a thin consistency, except as noted.

YOU'LL ALSO NEED:

- 1 fat quarter (18" x 22" piece of fabric)
- ice cube tray   ■ 1" mop brush
- water-filled spray bottle   ■ plastic container

1. Fill a plastic container partway with water and add a few drops of red-violet paint. Dip the fabric into the water and remove it (a quick "dunk and lift" motion). Lay the fabric flat and allow it to dry thoroughly.

2. Fill one compartment of an ice cube tray partway with blue paint. Fill another compartment with violet paint.

3. Lay the fabric flat, fan-fold it, and roll it up. Dip one end of the fabric roll into the blue paint—the walls of the compartment will hold it secure, so you won't need a rubber band. Let it sit 3–5 minutes, or until the fabric folds wick up some of the paint.

4. Dip the other end of the roll into violet paint. Remove after 3–5 minutes.

5. Undo the roll, open out the fabric, and lay it flat. Spritz with water to encourage color diffusion. Let dry.

6. Use a 1" mop brush to splatter light blue paint across the fabric surface. Let dry.

DESIGN TIP: USE OPAQUE PAINT TO SPLATTER LIGHT COLORS ACROSS A DARK SURFACE. TRANSPARENT PAINTS WILL NOT SHOW UP AGAINST A DARKER BACKGROUND.

BOUND AND STITCHED RESIST

In these techniques, strong thread is used to bind or gather a piece of fabric. Paint finds it hard, but not impossible, to reach the constricted areas. Tight bindings and medium-viscosity paint help ensure that the resist effect is not lost.

■ **GATHERED RESIST** Fold a piece of dry or wet fabric diagonally or crosswise, slip a strong, heavy thread inside the fold, and then fold or roll the fabric around this thread core. Draw the ends of the thread together to form a fabric ring and tie tightly.

The gathered ring can be painted using a brush or a sponge. Don't forget to paint both sides. Place the painted ring on a flat surface to dry. Remember that the wet paint will diffuse downward; the paint at the top will diffuse more than that on the bottom.

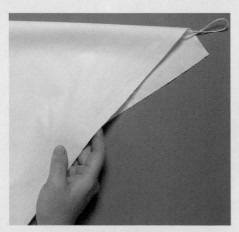
Place the thread inside the fold.

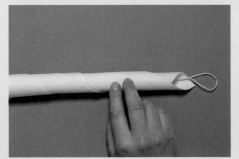
Gather and tie to form a ring.

Roll the fabric around the thread.

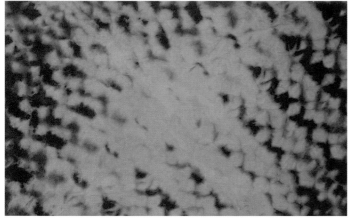

Diagonal Gathers on Dry Fabric

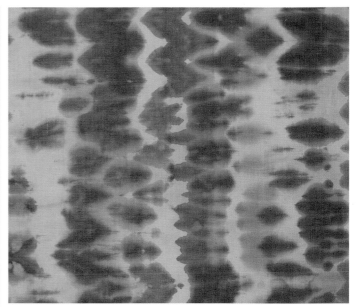

Fanfolded and Wrapped—Dry

The bundle can be dry or wet when you paint it, with widely varying results.

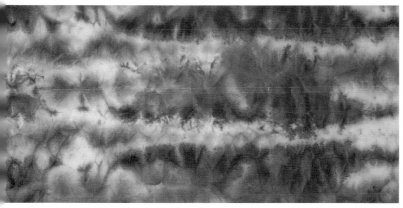

Horizontal Gathers on Wet Fabric

■ **WRAPPED RESIST** In this technique, the fabric is folded, gathered, or rolled and then tightly wrapped with thread at various intervals along its length. The wrapped fabric can be painted with a brush or a sponge. Different colored stripes, painted either across or diagonally, give particularly interesting effects. Remember to paint both sides.

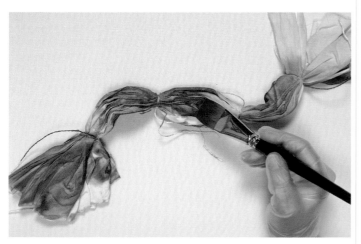

Gather the fabric, tie with thread, and paint.

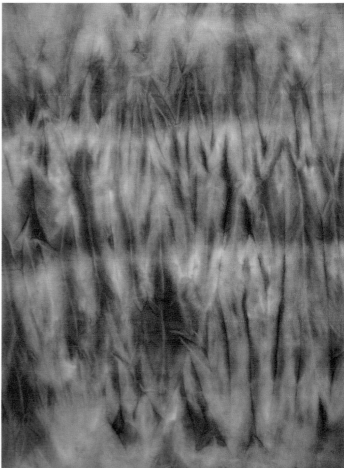

Gathered and Wrapped—Wet

A variation of this technique is to start the wrapping process in the middle of the fabric. Lay the fabric flat, grab and pinch the middle, and lift up, so that the fabric drapes down in loose vertical folds. Lay the draped fabric on a horizontal surface, and bind it with thread at varying intervals. Painting will produce a radiating pattern, reminiscent of tie-dyeing.

Wrapping from the Middle

■ **BOUND RESIST** In this technique, the fabric is folded multiple times to make a small square or triangular bundle. The corners of the bundle are tightly bound with thread.

Bind the folded bundles at the corners and paint.

Soak the bundle in water until it is thoroughly dampened. Apply paint to the top of the bundle, and give it a few minutes to migrate down through the fabric layers. The wetter the fabric, the more readily the paint will migrate. Then flip the bundle over and paint the other side. Once again, give the paint time to migrate downward. Remove the bindings, open out the fabric, and lay it flat to dry.

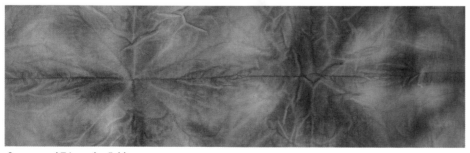

Square and Triangular Folds

■ **PINCHED RESIST** In this variation, small sections of fabric are pinched and tied. The spacing between the bound tufts can vary.

Tie off small "pinches" of fabric.

Dampen the fabric thoroughly and spread it out, creating folds and creases between the tufts. Lightly brush medium to thick paint across the top of the creases. Avoid using thin paint—it will seep down into the folds, and the effect will not be as obvious. You can also splash the paint onto the surface.

Splashing over Pinched Bindings

For a quick and easy variation, add a few drops of Pebeo paint to a container of water. Dip the fabric in the water and lay it outside to dry, allowing the wrinkles to sunprint.

Pinched and Sunprinted

■ **STITCHED RESIST** In this technique, fabric is stitched, tightly gathered, and painted. Small dots appear along the stitching line where the compressed fabric resists the paint. It's a fascinating visual effect.

To machine-stitch your fabric, select a straight stitch with the longest stitch length possible. Use quilting thread or another strong thread in the bobbin; this is the thread you will pull to make the gathers. If you are hand-stitching your fabric, use quilting thread or something slightly heavier. Don't go too heavy, though—you don't want holes in your fabric after the thread is removed.

The stitching can take a straight line, form a circle or grid, or meander at random. Be aware that stitching lines that cross each other will be more difficult to gather.

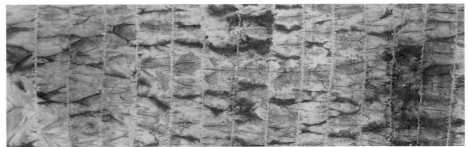

Straight Stitching Lines

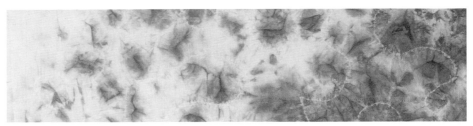

Meandering Stitching

Pull one end of the thread and draw it up tightly to gather the fabric. The fabric must be very tightly constricted. If you can't pull the entire length of thread, cut it, tie it off, and start again with a new section.

The Perfect Backyard, Gail Strout, 2003, 39³/4" x 35". Machine-pieced, hand-quilted.

Once your fabric has been gathered, it is ready to paint. Gathered fabric can bulk up quite a bit. You can paint both sides. The colors do not have to be the same, but remember that they will blend.

Stitch meandering lines.

Draw up the thread to gather the fabric.

Here are some variations to try:

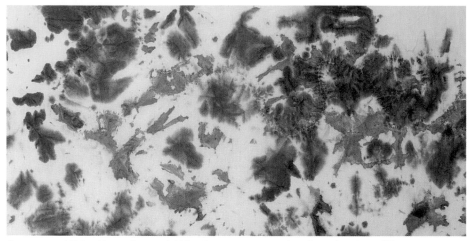

Concentrated Color. Use medium and thick paints to concentrate the color and minimize diffusion.

Selected Diffusion. Spritz the fabric after painting.

Full Diffusion. Soak the gathered fabric in water before painting.

Remember that paint will migrate downward while drying. The paint on the top of the fabric will diffuse more than that on the bottom. Do not remove the stitches until the fabric has dried.

RINGSIDE

An understated checked pattern is created by rolling and tying a fabric bundle. The effect is enhanced with stenciled squares.

Prepare your color palette:

- green (medium, must be able to sunprint)
- dark blue (medium)
- blue (thick, transparent)
- white (thick, opaque)

  Make various consistencies, as noted.

YOU'LL ALSO NEED:

- 1 fat quarter (18" x 22" piece of fabric)
- stencil: $5/8$" x $5/8$" squares in a random grid
- 1" flat watercolor brush
- strong thread   ■ plastic container

1. Fill a plastic container partway with water. Add a few drops of green paint. Dip the fabric into the solution, remove promptly, and gently wring out the excess moisture. Dry in full sun to allow the fabric to sunprint.

2. Lay the dry fabric flat, fold it in half diagonally, and slip a length of strong thread inside the fold. Roll the fabric around the thread. Tie the ends of the thread together tightly, gathering the fabric into a ring.

3. Soak the fabric ring in a container of water until thoroughly damp. Gently wring out the excess moisture. Use a 1" flat watercolor brush to apply dark blue paint to the fabric ring. Undo the ring and lay the fabric flat to dry.

4. Use the stencil and a 1" flat watercolor brush to paint transparent blue squares in the green areas. Stencil opaque white and dark blue squares, mixing the colors slightly, in the darker areas. Lay the fabric flat until dry.

> ⊞ **STENCIL TIP:** WHEN PAINT COLORS ARE MIXED SLIGHTLY, NOT THOROUGHLY, THERE IS MORE VARIETY IN THE PAINTED SURFACE. SOMETIMES ONE COLOR WILL SHOW MORE THAN THE OTHER. THIS EFFECT ADDS VISUAL DEPTH TO THE STENCILING.

TORTOISESHELL

Painting each side of a fabric bundle creates a dense visual effect with minimal effort.

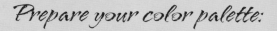

Prepare your color palette:

■ yellow   ■ yellow-orange   ■ red-orange
Make all a medium consistency.

YOU'LL ALSO NEED:
■ 1 fat quarter (18" x 22" piece of fabric)
■ 1" flat watercolor brush
■ thread
■ plastic containers

1. Fill a container partway with water. Add a few drops of yellow paint. Dip the fabric into the solution, wring out the excess moisture, and lay it flat to dry.

2. Fold the fabric in half, and then in half again, for a piece that is almost square. Fold one corner (all 4 layers) onto the opposite corner, making a triangle.

3. Position the triangle on the work surface so that the long edge faces you. Bring the 2 lower triangle points up to the top point—first the lower left point and then the lower right point—to make a small square set on point. Tightly bind the top and bottom points of the square with thread to keep the folds from flopping open.

4. Soak the bundle in a container of water until thoroughly dampened. Squeeze out the excess moisture. Use a 1" flat watercolor brush to apply yellow-orange paint to the underside (the plain side) of the bundle. Flip the bundle over and paint the top (folded) side red-orange. Let the bundle sit, red-orange side up, for 15 minutes, or until the paint partially absorbs.

5. Untie and remove the bindings. Unfold the fabric and lay it flat to dry.

BINDING TIP: THE TIGHTER THE BINDINGS, THE LESS THE PAINT IS ABLE TO SEEP BENEATH THEM. THE TIGHT BINDINGS, FOLDING, AND PAINTING WORK TOGETHER TO CREATE THE EFFECT.

Paint Comparison Chart

	GOLDEN FLUID ACRYLIC	PEBEO SETACOLOR TEXTILE PAINT	PROFAB TEXTILE PAINT	PROFAB COLOR CONCENTRATES
COLOR RANGE	51 colors 10 iridescent colors 10 interference colors	21 transparent and opaque colors opaque shimmer and fluorescent colors also available	45 transparent and opaque colors 12 pearl colors 6 fluorescent colors	17 transparent and opaque colors
CONSISTENCY	medium	thin to medium	thick	thick
THINNING AGENTS	GAC 900 (1:1 ratio) Water	Water (1:1 ratio)	LoCrock solution (1:1 ratio) Water (1:1 ratio)	LoCrock solution (add 1 tsp. to 8 tsp. color concentrate to 1 cup LoCrock solution; can be further thinned with water)
THICKENING AGENTS	Silk Screen Fabric Gel (1:1 ratio)	Thickener. Add a few drops at a time while stirring constantly. Achieves modest thickening only.	None required; use in original consistency.	PROfab Base Extender (add 1 tsp. to 8 tsp. color concentrate to 1 cup PROfab Base Extender)
COLOR SETTING TIME	1 day (before heat setting)	Air-dry thoroughly (before heat setting)	Air-dry thoroughly (before heat setting)	Air-dry thoroughly (before heat setting)
IRON HEAT SET	3 to 5 minutes, medium to hot iron	3 to 4 minutes, medium to hot iron	5 minutes, hot iron	5 minutes, hot iron
OVEN HEAT SET	Not recommended by manufacturer	No manufacturer recommendation	Roll in newsprint* and place in oven 2 to 3 minutes at 350°F	Roll in newsprint* and place in oven 2 to 3 minutes at 350°F
CLOTHES DRYER HEAT SET	30 minutes, hottest setting	60 to 90 minutes, hottest setting	60 to 90 minutes hottest setting	60 to 90 minutes, hottest setting
PASSIVE SET	Let sit 7 to 10 days before washing	No manufacturer's recommendation	Let sit 10 to 14 days before washing	Let sit 10 to 14 days before washing
LAUNDERING	Allow 2 days after heat setting. Hand-wash, line-dry.	Allow 2 days after heat setting. Hand-wash, line-dry.	Allow 10 to 14 days after heat setting. Hand-wash, line-dry.	Allow 10 to 14 days after heat setting. Hand-wash, line-dry.
COMMENTS	• Beautiful, clear colors • Can achieve a very dilute color without pigment particle separation. • Fully saturated low-value colors generally make the fabric stiff when used in large areas.	• Maintains good low-value color saturation when paint is thinned. • Impossible to achieve very thick consistency • Add Lightening Medium (1:1 ratio) to raise the value without changing the viscosity.	• Maintains excellent low-value color saturation when paint is thinned. • Add PROfab Base Extender (1:1 ratio) or white to raise the value without changing the consistency.	• Paint has no affinity for fabric without addition of LoCrock solution or PROfab Base Extender. • Maintains excellent low-value color saturation when paint is thinned.

*Newsprint is a thin paper sold at art supply stores. Do not use newspaper, as the print will rub off.

Troubleshooting

Even with a freestyle approach to painting, problems do occur. Here are some common problems, their probable causes, and solutions to get you back on track.

PROBLEM	CAUSE	SOLUTION
A "dusty" appearance	A large pigment particle has separated out of very dilute paint (generally occurs with Pebeo paint).	• Use white paint instead of water to achieve a light color. • Use Golden Fluid Acrylic paint. Mix the desired color. Allow it to sit 15 to 20 minutes before applying. • Use PROfab color concentrate thinned with LoCrock solution.
Large, dark areas have a "fuzzy" appearance.	Paint has not colored the entire fiber surface. This generally occurs when the brush or sponge doesn't rub over the fabric surface, such as in walling-in, dipping, and confined color mixing.	Gently rub the brush over the painted areas of the fabric, especially where the paint is darkest.
	Fabric has been machine-washed.	Hand-launder fabric in warm, not hot, water.
Colors turn muddy where they diffuse and mix together.	Complementary colors or two or more toned colors were used.	• Spot-dry the first color before applying the second color. • Use opaque colors. • Use thicker paint. Thick paint does not diffuse as easily as thin paint. • Paint on dry fabric to discourage diffusion and blending.
The salting effect is not very pronounced.	Paint consistency is too thick.	Use thinner paint.
	Paint is too dry. Paint particles cannot migrate toward the salt particle.	Lightly spritz the fabric prior to salting to provide more moisture.
	Too much moisture is in the air.	• Wait for dry, sunny day. • Use a fan to circulate the air.
	Too little salt was used.	Apply salt more generously.
	Salt particles are too close together or concentrated in one area.	Sprinkle salt lightly over the entire fabric.
A blotch forms under a stencil or mask.	Too much paint is used.	Load the brush lightly and wipe off the excess.
	The stencil or mask is not adhering properly.	• Make sure the fabric is dry. • Make sure the stencil or mask is not warped. • Work on a flat surface.
	Paint is too thin.	Thicken the paint to a medium to thick consistency.

Materials and Supplies

The paints and artist's brushes recommended in this book are available at art supply stores or through the vendors listed below. General supplies are as close as your nearest supermarket, hardware store, or home improvement center.

Golden Artists Colors
188 Bell Road
New Berlin, NY 13411
607-847-6154
fax: 607-847-9336
www.goldenpaints.com

PRO Chemical and Dye Inc.
P.O. Box 14
Somerset, MA 02726
Orders: 1-800-2-BUY-DYE
Technical support: 508-676-3838
Fax: 508-676-3980
www.prochemical.com

Evening, Sue Beevers, 2000, 35" x 42". Hand- and machine-pieced, machine-quilted.

About the Author

Sue Beevers is both a musician and a visual artist. A cellist, she also loves to draw and paint and has been immersed for the past 30-plus years in the fiber field, first as a weaver, spinner, and dyer and now as a fabric painter and quilter. She has taught weaving, spinning, and dyeing classes and conducted workshops throughout the United States and at major fiber conferences. Her work is featured in collections in the United States, Europe, and Japan.

Sue first began painting fabric that she had woven herself. Painting proved such an interesting visual, she was soon concentrating less on the weaving and more on the painting. Today, she paints almost exclusively on commercially made fabrics. Many of her pieces have been matted and framed, to be viewed as works of art on the wall.

Painted fabrics led Sue to discover quilting, an art form she approaches much the way she does collage. Sue's painted and quilted themes revolve around people, nature, and the natural cycles of the earth. Other artists use Sue's painted fabrics to express their own, sometimes very different, design visions, an extension that Sue finds fascinating.

In *Off-the-Shelf Fabric Painting*, Sue Beevers shares her techniques, recipes, and tips for this wonderfully expressive art form in a way that everyone can enjoy.

Index

Forest, Gail Strout, 2002, 26" x 29". Machine-pieced, machine-quilted.